publishing

John T. Wilson

TEACH YOURSELF BOOKS

For UK order queries: please contact Bookpoint Ltd, 130 Milton Park, Abingdon, Oxon OX14 48B. Telephone: (44) 01235 827720. Fax: (44) 01235 400454. Lines are open from 9.00–18.00, Monday to Saturday, with a 24-hour message answering service. Email address: orders@bookpoint.co.uk

For U.S.A. order queries: please contact McGraw-Hill Customer Services, P.O. Box 545, Blacklick, OH 43004-0545, U.S.A. Telephone: 1-800-722-4726. Fax: 1-614-755-5645.

For Canada order queries: please contact McGraw-Hill Ryerson Ltd., 300 Water St, Whitby, Ontario L1N 9B6, Canada. Telephone: 905 430 5000. Fax: 905 430 5020.

Long renowned as the authoritative source for self-guided learning – with more than 30 million copies sold worldwide – the *Teach Yourself* series includes over 300 titles in the fields of languages, crafts, hobbies, business and education.

British Library Cataloguing in Publication Data
A catalogue record for this title is available from The British Library.

Library of Congress Catalog Card Number: On file

First published in UK 2001 by Hodder Headline Plc, 338 Euston Road, London, NW1 3BH.

First published in US 2001 by Contemporary Books, A Division of The McGraw-Hill Companies, 4255 West Touhy Avenue, Lincolnwood (Chicago), Illinois 60712–1975 U.S.A.

The 'Teach Yourself' name and logo are registered trade marks of Hodder & Stoughton Ltd.

Copyright © 2001 John T. Wilson

Typeset by Transet Limited, Coventry, England.
Printed in Great Britain for Hodder & Stoughton Educational, a division of Hodder Headline Plc, 338 Euston Road, London NW1 3BH by Cox & Wyman Ltd, Reading, Berkshire.

Impression number   10 9 8 7 6 5 4 3 2 1
Year   2007 2006 2005 2004 2003 2002 2001

CONTENTS

PREFACE

Crammed full of practical help and advice from the author's two decades of experience as a small-scale publisher and including lots of sources of additional information, supplies and services complete with names, addresses, telephone numbers, e-mail and website addresses, *Teach Yourself Publishing* offers readers the guidance and know-how to become small-scale publishers themselves for fun or profit – or both – with 30 practical project ideas for setting up a small publishing business of their own with minimal capital.

John Wilson

22 August 1940–14 February 2001

John was born in Paisley in Scotland. He left school at 15 but went on to finish his education as a mature student at Strathclyde University gaining a BA (Hons) and also an MA. He became a lecturer in English at Leeds and Wakefield and finally became the youngest Principal to run a large and busy Adult Education Centre in Gravesend, Kent. It was during the 1970s that he first became interested in publishing, producing a book of poetry for the Victoria Centre. He published a number of books for other authors as well as having many of his own books published and in 1986 started the 'Escape Committee' newsletter for teachers. We moved to Cornwall in 1987 where John was able to continue with his newsletter as well as writing articles and reports for other people. He was a prolific writer and was extremely well regarded in the writing and publishing industry. Always being interested in the small business field he started another newsletter called 'Great Ideas'. He was well known for his kindness and encouragement, sincerity and absolute professionalism. As someone said at his memorial service 'he was a very decent man'.

He is sadly missed by myself, our family, friends and everyone who had contact with him.

Sue Wilson

1 | PUBLISHING OPPORTUNITIES

Can publishing make you rich?

Yes, publishing can make you seriously rich. Michael Heseltine made his wealth from setting up a small magazine company which became very successful and turned into a large publishing conglomerate. Rupert Murdoch has become rich beyond belief from owning newspapers and other complex publishing businesses. Lord Stockton's fortune was made from the Macmillan publishing empire started by his great grandfather who began life as a crofter in the Scottish island of Arran.

Thousands of people have made fortunes, become seriously rich or made a more than comfortable living from the publishing business. What about you? Can you do the same?

Can *you* become a publisher?

Of course you can, but it's not guaranteed. Just as in any sphere of business endeavour some people make it big from small beginnings, some have better entrepreneurial skills than others, and some get lucky, while others have a run of bad luck. So, yes, you could be one of publishing's brightly shining success stories in the future. On the other hand you may simply become one of the many people who make a reasonable to good living doing something which most of them, whatever level of success they experience, will tell you is both enjoyable and satisfying.

Before you can judge whether or not you have a chance to become rich through publishing, you need to answer the more basic question of whether you can actually become a publisher. Isn't publishing a highly specialist job in which you have to have training and experience of the kind acquired in Fleet Street or Bloomsbury? Don't you have to serve an apprenticeship in a newspaper or magazine office or in the rarefied atmosphere of a prestigious publishing house?

Of course that kind of background is invaluable; however, three things suggest that you can do just as well without it. The first is that a background in corporate publishing can actually be inhibiting to setting up a smaller enterprise. Functions are separated and specialized and the scale of operation is so large and complex that it can be daunting to consider doing it all yourself as an independent. The second is that the technologies involved in publishing, from the origination of the words on paper to layout, printing, distribution and marketing, have advanced so fast in the last few years that it has become possible for one person, with the appropriate tools, to originate, typeset, print, bind, market and distribute a publication or range of publications from a desk at home. This book will show you how to do that. Thirdly, methods for the dissemination of information to other people (the process that we call publishing) have become so varied that conventional publishing in the form of hardback and paperback books or newspapers and magazines distributed through retail bookshops and newsagents has become only a part of a wider spectrum of activities. Publishing now encompasses the use of media such as audio and video tapes, newsletters run off on a photocopier or digital printer, books on computer disk, information accessed through dedicated telephone lines and information disseminated through the internet on websites or by the use of e-mail. All of these media and their use are explored in this book.

Despite the increase in television viewing, the growth of computer ownership and the phenomenal explosion of the internet as alternative means of distribution of information, learning and entertainment, there has been no diminution of the numbers of books published, with year by year growth. The demise in the UK of the Net Book Agreement (a retail price maintenance agreement which prevented books being discounted until fairly recently) and the availability of discounted books through internet booksellers like Amazon, has meant that even more books are sold than before. As a wise man once said, 'Of making many books there is no end' (*Ecclesiastes* 12:12).

Clearly a publishing boom such as we are seeing brings opportunities. If more books are being written, published, bought and read then there are more opportunities for writers to benefit by producing those books. But it also means increased opportunities for small publishers, for new publishing houses setting out and for the growing army of self-publishing writers who are able to use the new technologies available to produce their own books (and other publishing products) in reasonable numbers and at low cost and thus take charge of their own destinies as writer-publishers.

These new technologies have themselves fuelled a boom in 'alternative' publishing, from newsletters and magazines, to short-run paperbacks, electronic books, e-zines and internet publishing, so that anyone with a message or story to communicate – or who simply has the business acumen to want to tap into the profits that such low-cost publishing opportunities offer – can become a publisher with a home-based PC and low-cost laser printer or an internet connection or other appropriate equipment.

How publishing works

Before taking a look at the widely varied possibilities now open to the tyro (novice) publisher, it might be useful to have a brief overview of how mainstream publishing works.

A book begins as an idea originating from a writer or by a commissioning editor who will then approach one of the publishing house's writers to develop the idea. The writer then prepares a synopsis of the proposed book with an overview of the rationale of the book – that is, why such a book is needed or will meet a perceived demand, together with some indication of the potential market for the title. A sample chapter will invariably accompany this analysis, particularly if the idea is one that originates with a writer who then submits it to a publishing house to see if they are interested in taking it on board.

Depending on the procedure followed by that particular publisher, the commissioning editor will then submit the synopsis and sample chapter to one or two readers chosen for their knowledge or experience of the subject area of the book. These readers then submit reports and recommendations which will form part of the editor's decision as to whether to commission the book or not, resulting in either a letter to the writer declining the offer to publish or the offer of a contract.

The writer writes the book with as much editorial help, advice or interference as is the practice of that particular publisher and eventually the manuscript is handed over (usually on computer disk as well as in manuscript form) for approval and acceptance. The publishing process takes over from here.

In brief, the manuscript is checked and edited for style and grammatical correctness and is then sent to a typesetter – usually independent of the publishing house – and decisions are made about cover or jacket design, print run, promotion and publicity and so on. Finally the first run of the book is printed (again, usually by a specialist book printing company) and the book is launched to the retail trade to make its way against all the other thousands of titles competing for the attention of the fickle public or specialist market. If the writer and publisher are lucky (or, as they may argue, if their skill and judgement have produced the right book for the market) then the book goes into further editions and both writer and publisher make money.

The above abbreviated account of the publishing process leaves out many of the more complex aspects, but it does begin to show that getting a book published successfully through conventional or mainstream publishing channels can be hazardous and fraught with all sorts of delays, problems and threats to the eventual success of the title. That is why, of course, publishers hedge their bets by publishing a large number of books, only some of which will become the money-earning stars while others don't do so well, picking up small sales and fading out of the publisher's list in a fairly short time. If one of these also-rans is your book, you will feel somewhat aggrieved. By becoming your own publisher you may do much better – though there are pitfalls and you may not do nearly as well as you imagine without the expertise and back-up of a large publisher with their professional sales and distribution resources. So, what are the chances that you can do better by doing it yourself?

A different kind of publishing

The answer to that question is, better than you might imagine – provided that you don't try to operate in the same way as the big publishing houses and take note of the advice and help in the further chapters of this book. Many people who decide to publish their own book think that writing and producing the book is the major part of publishing. It isn't. The publisher's real job is just beginning at this point. What is the good of producing 2,000 copies of a hardback book that have cost you £4 a copy to produce when, after a couple of years of intense and expensive efforts to sell them you still have 1,723 sitting in boxes in your garage? The £3,325 you have gathered in on sales of 277 books at £12 a copy don't even begin to cover your production costs, never mind your overheads for sales and distribution. What is more, if you have sold, say, 200 of these books through the retail book trade you will have had to give a 35 per cent discount, reducing your total gathered in through sales to £2,484. Publishing successfully and *profitably* is not as easy as many people think. You have to learn a different kind of publishing. What is that different kind of publishing?

You might call it guerrilla publishing – learning to duck and dive and skirmish and come out alive! The first thing you have to take on board is that in this different kind of publishing you are not in the business of aping the big publishers, but in doing things in a different way entirely – a way that is appropriate to your circumstances, your objectives and your finances.

In the main you will be practising a kind of publishing which:

- aims at niche markets
- produces short-run publications
- operates from a home base
- relies on direct sales of some kind or another
- uses simple but effective technologies in print and non-print media
- focuses on publishing-on-demand without having to keep large stocks
- makes its profits from further sales to buyers.

What you will *not* be doing, in all probability, is publishing novels or fiction or books of poetry (unless it is low-brow, popular or humorous) or a wide-ranging general list. It is also unlikely that you will be publishing traditional hardback books – perhaps not even paperbacks, though the technologies that allow very small numbers of paperbacks to be produced may make this feasible in some circumstances. You may be producing photocopied comb-bound books, simple photocopied or digitally printed newsletters or magazines, books and other information products on computer disk, information on cassettes or videos, card or poster based items, or information products that sit in your computer or website until a sale is made and the item is transmitted electronically (virtually no product costs at all!). Once you have built up some experience and expertise you may be doing all or some of these things for other people for a fee, leaving them with the hardest part of publishing – or indeed any business – that of marketing the goods and getting sales.

If it all sounds rather daunting, don't let it put you off. Most of what we are describing is really quite straightforward once you know what to do. Later chapters will cover all you need to know and may even give you some ideas for projects you could pick up and get started on straightaway so that you, too, can make money from publishing.

2 | BUSINESS BASICS

Publishing is a business like any other and must be run on a proper, businesslike basis. While attending to the details of book-keeping systems and dealing with banks and accountants may seem dull and boring, unless you get the nuts and bolts of your business right at the beginning you may find it falling apart once the realities of business start to put pressure on the ramshackle edifice you have allowed to grow by default. A strong foundation at the beginning will prevent many structural problems in the future when you want to be devoting your energy to the development and growth of your business rather than sorting out problems that some forethought would have prevented in the first place. So, spend some time on getting the business set up on a sound administrative and professional basis before you do anything else. This chapter focuses on the major areas you will need to consider.

Your vision or purpose

Every business starts from an idea. That idea may be as mundane as 'I'd like to run my own business' or as specific as 'I'd like to teach everyone in the world my new method of playing the mouth organ'. Your vision may be commonplace or unique. You may simply want to earn more money, be independent, become very rich, make your mark on the world, run the best specialist publishing house in the world, promote your own writings or be at the forefront of the electronic publishing revolution. What is your vision? Stop for a few moments now and write down what it is you want to achieve with your business. (It's a good idea to buy a special, robust notebook to write down your ideas, work out figures and keep notes about everything to do with your business, then you won't find yourself looking for an old envelope that you scribbled a vital phone number on!) Write down in your notebook why you want to run your own business, what you will be doing and what you think it will be like. Having a clear idea of what your vision or what the point and purpose of your business is will focus your mind and enable you to see clearly what needs to be done to make your vision a reality and to plan your business effectively.

What do you know?

Some people know exactly what their business is going to be. They know that they want to publish poetry, publish books for others on a contract basis, or sell information manuals by mail order, for example. In some ways they are lucky; they don't have to think through the thousands of possibilities that would otherwise be open to them, making choice difficult. On the other hand, they are subject to the very real danger of being blinded by their enthusiasm to some of the realities of business. Their enthusiasm and commitment may lead them to ignore the fact that their potential market is too limited or too expensive to reach, or some other negative aspect that might warn a more objective entrepreneur that the business would present difficulties which may not be easy to overcome. Enthusiasm can overcome many problems that a more hard-headed business approach would consider insurmountable, and there are plenty of examples of enthusiasts who have carried off the most unlikely publishing successes by sheer dogged persistence arising from a love of what they are engaged in, where others would have given up and opened a beauty parlour instead.

Having said that, it is sensible to make your present knowledge and experience the first thing to explore in the search for a business vision or publishing purpose. If you have spent many years in horticulture or education, for example, you have obvious skills and knowledge that could be a sound basis for a publishing business focusing on those areas. Perhaps you have a clear idea of how gardening knowledge can be marketed more effectively using video 'books' on the back of the gardening television programmes that are so popular these days. Your educational experience might lead you to offer a new kind of educational multi-media pack for schools or a specialist newsletter or magazine for teachers or pupils.

Don't forget, when listing your areas of knowledge and skill, to put down those you may not be consciously aware of – being good with people, being a good listener, good at DIY, good at fixing cars, interested in wildlife and so on. Some of these less-recognized skills and interests may turn out to be the very thing that will give you the idea for a publishing business you would not otherwise have thought of.

Go beyond your range of current knowledge and skills to explore new possibilities. Read widely, think laterally and write down in your business notebook any mad ideas that occur to you, any business fantasy that appeals. Write down ideas for categories of books that people haven't thought of yet, needs that you observe locally, problems that need to be solved, people who want to change things in their lives, information you think people might need as the world changes. Think of crazy ideas like borrow a granny, rent a brain, share a boat, swap a skill, timeshare a caravan, community cars, a dining club for bored couples, an OAP dating service and so on – ideas that might lend themselves to new-style publishing guides in book, audio tape or other format. The possibilities are limited only by your fertile brain and your lurid imagination! And it is out of such 'thinking outside the box' that some of the great publishing ideas have come.

So, get to work on your vision. Decide what your ultimate business objective will be. If you can't, and think, 'I'd just like to do my own thing' or 'I'd just like to earn some extra money', then that's fine. Once you get started you will find that bigger ideas will come and a surer direction will emerge from your tentative beginnings. Then you can go through this 'vision thing' and your purposes will become clearer.

Business goals and target market

Assuming that you have some idea of what your business purpose or vision is (even if it is just to earn more money or be independent), it is a good idea to set down on paper some basic goals for your publishing business. These might be as simple as 'to get my business up and running' or 'to publish my first book' or ' to earn enough to pay the mortgage and other living expenses'. Don't make the mistake of setting goals that are too ambitious and therefore unlikely to be reached, as this is setting yourself up for failure. Set goals which are realistic and realizable – you can always set higher goals once you have achieved the more easily attainable ones. Also, it is important to write them down as this helps you to commit to them and gives a written yardstick by which to measure achievement. Your goals should be specific, so that they are objectively measurable and they should be things you really want to achieve rather than goals which are set by other people's agendas or that you think you ought to want to achieve.

The achievement of your business goals is tied, inevitably, to your market. If you don't sell enough of your books, or if your newsletter isn't in demand, you won't do enough business and your goals will not be fulfilled. Before your business begins you need to do some preliminary assessment of the potential market for your intended publishing product. Is there a market for it at all? Are other people operating in the same market? Are they flourishing? Is there scope in that marketplace for a fresh approach, new services, a different way of tapping the market? Beware the alluring thought that says because no one is targeting the market you envisage tapping into, it must be rich, virgin territory that will produce masses of sales and make you rich. It is highly unlikely that the market has not been explored before; far more likely that others have tried it and found that the market is unresponsive or that offerings of the kind you envisage are not wanted. Let others' experience be your guide to the general existence of a market of the kind you seek – don't make the mistake of thinking that you can succeed where others have failed. It is possible, but unlikely, and horribly expensive if you have made a disastrous mistake.

Hobby or business

Many people who run a small publishing business prefer to earn their living by a full-time job and simply enjoying their publishing as a very interesting part-time and (hopefully) paying hobby. Others take the same route, but from a different perspective, either seeing their part-time publishing venture as a way of increasing their earnings or as a stepping stone to a full-time business when it reaches the point of being able to replace their full-time job. What you want from your small publishing venture is *your* decision, though you will probably find that your ideas will change and develop as your venture grows. Your business may be so successful that it will dictate that you give up your full-time job to develop it into a fully-fledged publishing house.

Trading name and style

Of course there is no reason why you should not trade under your own name – and that is certainly the simplest option: John Bloggs, Publisher is as good a name as any and there are fewer complications. However, many would argue that a good name enhances the business and can be a useful indicator of the kind of publishing you are engaged in. West Highland Books, for example, clearly indicates a regional flavour and the even more specific name West Highland Wildlife Books means fewer hopeful authors or misguided readers wasting their time and yours, asking if you publish books on Dorset or train spotting. Unless you have a very clear vision of where your publishing interests lie in the beginning, however, you may want to opt for a name with more generic possibilities: Cornucopia Press or Panache Publishing would be names that would not inhibit publishing any kind of book or other media in just about any subject, which carries the advantage that you can change direction or diversify any time the need arises. Note, however, that while you do not have to register the name of an unincorporated business, there are nonetheless some legal restrictions on names which you can use. Some names require the approval of the relevant government department and there are certain words which must not be used (such as Royal, UK, Prince, US), offensive names should be avoided, and there are words for which permission must be sought from the relevant body before they can be used in a business name. These include: Association, British, English, European, Group, Holding, Institute, National, International, Society, Trust, United Kingdom, etc. (*Business Names Act*, 1985, Section 3). These same rules apply to limited companies and other business formats too.

Structure

More important is the choice of trading structure. What choices are there?

You can run your publishing enterprise as a sole trader, which is just you trading under your own or a designated name. It can be run as a partnership of two or more people, which can have the advantage of sharing diverse skills, but can also lead to problems. Bear in mind that partners are individually responsible for the actions of any other member of the partnership and disputes can arise which can wreck friendships or marriages, never mind the business partnership in which they are involved. There can be problems of inheritance, the sale of a partner's share or division of responsibilities or rewards. If you decide to run as a partnership – even with your best friend, spouse or life-partner – do get a partnership agreement drawn up with the help of a lawyer. Business divorce can be as messy and painful as marital separation – and just as costly!

A co-operative is a possible structure, probably best for a non-profit making enterprise or one where strongly egalitarian principles underpin the philosophy of the participants. Co-operatives can be set up as partnerships or as limited companies and are subject to the same legal rules and constraints that govern these types of business structure.

A company-based structure is often chosen because a company has a separate legal identity from the owners or shareholders whose financial and legal responsibilities are limited and their personal assets and finances protected in the event of failure. In practice it is, however, not as simple as it appears, for unless the company itself owns assets such as a building or equipment which can be held as security for borrowings and debts, then it is likely that the directors will have to give the bank personal guarantees, usually based on the value of their home or other personal assets, which defeats the objective. Directors can also be held legally liable if they have conducted themselves in a way detrimental to the well-being of the business.

Since 6 April 2001 a new legal format has come into being (in the UK), the Limited Liability Partnership, which gives a more secure structure for partnerships, mitigating some of the disadvantages of partnerships and offering some of the advantages secured by the Limited Company set-up.

The question of which business structure is appropriate to your publishing enterprise is one which depends to a large extent on size and scope and which needs to be discussed with your accountant. However, the only real advantage of a company for the new publishing start-up is that it may confer a certain amount of credibility, but at the expense of being the most tax efficient structure, which is usually the status of sole trader or partnership. The Limited Liability Partnership may prove to be just the kind of structure the smaller business enterprise requires.

Stationery

Every business needs stationery and it is perhaps one of the first excitements of the embryonic business when you collect a set of letterheads, compliments slips and other items from your printer: somehow, your venture begins to seem real from that point. Go for a style which is simple and classic, easy to read and printed on good quality paper. An appropriate and well-designed company logo can help enormously to establish the kind of memorable image you want your publishing enterprise to have. Bear in mind that if you are trading as a sole trader or partnership under any name(s) other than your own, that the name of the proprietor(s) must appear on the letterhead, while on a company letterhead the name(s) of the director(s) should appear together with the company's registration number and registered address.

Professional help and advice

Clearly contact with some professional advisers will be more immediately necessary than others and much will depend on the nature and development of your business.

Lawyers

While most business books will recommend that your new business will need a solicitor, it is my experience that a micro-business in almost any field will seldom need to consult a lawyer. In nearly 20 years of running my own small publishing business I have needed legal advice only twice and got that on one occasion from an informal but helpful chat on a possible libel issue with the Chairman of the Society of Authors to which I belonged at the time, consulting my family solicitor on another matter to do with the details of a contract I had entered into for the sale of two magazines we published. The exercise of care and common sense will obviate the need for expensive legal bills most of the time. Consult the law only when you need specific advice or help – and do it in plenty of time before you get into difficulties that will cost you a great deal to extricate yourself from.

Accountants

Whatever well-meaning friends may tell you, and allowing for the fact that you can do your own books, I would regard an accountant as *the* professional adviser you most definitely should engage. A good accountant will help you set up a book-keeping system that will be easy to run and helpful in managing your business, and will finalize your year-end accounts to save you from paying any more tax than you need to. In short, he or she will save you more than the few hundred pounds or dollars a year that you will pay in accountancy fees (which can, of course, be set against the expenses of doing business). You will get good advice on all aspects of taxation, how to benefit from structuring your financial year and how to make the most of claiming legitimate expenses to set against profits and protect your profits as far as legally possible.

Bank

You will need a bank to handle the money and financial transactions of your publishing business. Shop around for the best deal you can get, as banks often compete for new business by giving free banking for a period of time. Alternatively, try one of the many new internet or telephone-based banks.

Brokers

At this stage you won't need a broker to launch your new venture on the stock exchange, but there is a range of services for which you might need a broker – insurance, mortgages and pension, for example.

You need to consider what kind of insurance you need, particularly if you are working from home. Your household policy will not cover your business equipment or any public liability that may arise as a result of your business activities. In fact, your current insurance policies may be rendered invalid by the very fact of operating a business, however small, from your home. You might also like to consider taking out special insurance to cover libel claims against you as a publisher, though this is not cheap. Consider, too, that your mortgage or rent agreement may be breached by undertaking business activities. A remortgage could produce some of the capital you need for your business or for modifications and alterations to accommodate your business activities, and you may want to review your pension arrangements to add to them from your new business income or to replace existing arrangements with a new personal pension.

Marketing and PR professionals, copywriters, etc.

Experts proliferate to the extent that you sometimes feel that there is little left for you to do that they could not do better for you. It is my view, however, that functions such as marketing, public relations and copywriting, while highly skilled, are things that can be learnt, at least at a basic level, sufficiently well for the small publisher to do him- or herself. Later in this book we will be looking at the basics of all these skills so that you can do them yourself, bringing in a professional practitioner only for something special or highly critical.

Staff and other help

Similarly, it is unlikely that you will need to take on staff at an early stage of your publishing business. Bear in mind that while it is generally good advice to employ others to do what one colleague called '£4 an hour work' rather than tying yourself up doing mundane tasks, in the beginning you are probably better to be your own '£4 an hour' worker as well as doing the more significant and creative work. It is a known fact that those who run small businesses work extremely long hours, especially in the beginning. On another level it is perhaps important that you know every aspect of running your business, down to doing the photocopying and wrapping the parcels, so that when you do grow sufficiently to employ staff you will understand exactly what it is that you are asking them to do for their '£4 an hour'.

Legal matters

All UK businesses, particularly mail order based publishing, have an obligation to register under the Data Protection Act which regulates both computer held and paper-based records kept on customers. Broadly speaking, the act controls what data you can hold on customers and other contacts and what use you can put that to, and gives any individual the right to know what information you hold on him or her and to be removed from your mailing list if they so wish. Send for information to: The Data Protection Registrar, Wycliffe House, Water Lane, Wilmslow, Cheshire, SK9 5AF. Countries other than the UK will have their own equivalent legislation.

Keeping the books

Of course you need to keep good records for tax purposes, but a good system of book-keeping will help you to control and monitor your business not only at the end of the financial year, but on an on-going basis.

Your accountant will advise you as to how to set up the simplest system to meet both his and the tax authoritity's needs, but you must also work out what additional information you need to build into your system to provide the checks and information that will help you to keep track of what is happening and which of your publishing ventures are profitable.

While a fairly simple system that provides a record of what monies come in and what payments are made out, plus a record of what is going into the bank on a daily or weekly basis, is sufficient for most general purposes, it is helpful to have other columns in your books to split up the overall amounts and analyse them. You will want to be able to see at a glance how much you are spending under different headings on the expenses side. What are you spending on advertising? Are you overspending on packaging or are production costs spiralling out of control? Can you compare the expenditure on a particular aspect of the business (a newsletter, for example) with the income that it is producing? On the other hand it is important to know where your revenue is coming from and what is contributing the most to your profits – and that is not necessarily going to be the one that is bringing in the most money. Remember the Pareto Principle: 80 per cent of results tend to come from 20 per cent of the expenditure or effort. You need to be able to identify what is doing best and do more of it and cut back on those areas which take up a disproportionate amount of time, money and effort but contribute a relatively insignificant amount of the profits. That is what your books are for – not just so that you can pay the right amount of tax!

Other records and systems

You will need to think through how you intend to operate, what you intend to publish and how you are going to reach and interact with your customers, and then devise systems of record keeping and administration that will help the business to run smoothly. How will you keep control of stock? Will you need to keep records of authors and record royalty payments? What other aspects of the business will need to be administered and recorded to enable things to run smoothly? What procedures do you need to set up to deal efficiently and swiftly with orders? How will you keep track of work in progress? What delivery system will you use and how will you track orders? Many of these things will grow as the business develops, but it is important to think things through so that you have at least the beginnings of an efficient system in place.

Capital and other financial matters

You can start a publishing business with less than £100, or you can invest your redundancy money or the cash payout of your pension or your life savings, for example. Which you do will depend on your circumstances and personality, but if you have learning to do and that learning is going to be by experience – sometimes painful experience – then I advise caution in the first instance. Many of the publishing ideas you will find later in this book are deliberately low-cost projects and it is better to get one's hard experience and inevitable setbacks in a small low-cost project that neither breaks you nor breaks the bank so that you can dust yourself off, embrace the lessons you have learnt and carry on.

However, if you are going to run a serious business, you will need, at some point, to find some capital to fund your activities, as waiting for profits to accumulate is a slow business.

If you have savings, then clearly it makes sense to use those rather than borrow and have to pay interest, and if you have to borrow, make the bank the last port of call. You could take out a second mortgage on your home – but beware of the risk of losing your home if all goes wrong. Better still, a remortgage at preferential rates could give you a substantial sum for use in your business without costing you any more than you are paying out already.

Saving money is the best way of creating new capital and there are many ways in which your outgoings could be cut to provide quite substantial sums. Look at your mortgage and all insurance policies – life, car, household – as the premiums for these could be reduced considerably if you shop around for better deals. Any savings can then be diverted into the business, bringing a continuous flow of capital year on year.

If borrowing is a necessity, then it is often cheaper to borrow from an insurance company against an existing policy than to get a loan from the bank, and borrowing via a second mortgage or a remortgage is usually cheaper still. You could consider asking relatives or good friends if they would like to invest in your business in return for a modest rate of interest, a share in the business or a share in the profits. Alternatively, you could investigate whether any loans or grants are available through government or other agencies and, as a last resort you could approach your bank for a loan or a working overdraft.

Make sure that you make the best use of your money, borrowed or not. Keep it in an interest-bearing account until it is needed; don't spend it on kitting out the office with swanky new furniture or gadgets and gizmos. Put it to work in producing products and selling them.

Your business plan

You have got a business plan, haven't you? 'Of course I have!' you reply, 'only it's all in my head.' If that is the case, then you *haven't* got a business plan, only some hazy ideas! If you are going to be borrowing money from a bank (or even a relative) then you will have to do some hard work and put together a business plan of some kind. That plan will:

- identify the overall idea behind the business
- detail how that vision will translate into a practical course of action
- specify the products to be produced
- identify the markets and their characteristics
- outline the price structure of the product offerings, the costs of production, marketing and overheads
- provide a cash flow showing projected sales and estimated expenses
- contain all the other details about the business you can put together including a breakdown of the personnel involved (you and any others), their experience, skills and functions and how the whole business will work.

Take this plan to your accountant and let him or her ask you all the awkward questions you have fudged, tear your plan apart and rewrite it – then you will have a business plan. Don't file it – keep it on view and look at it and check progress with it every day so that you know if you are on target and, therefore, whether you will succeed.

3 | HOW TO GET STARTED

It has often been said that all a writer needs is a pen and a piece of paper. In a sense that is true, but to be a *successful* writer you need more: a computer, reference books, telephone, fax and, increasingly, internet access and an e-mail address. You don't get very far these days working on an old manual typewriter with misaligned keys and faded ribbon! Likewise, to be taken seriously as a publisher, even in a small way, you will need some minimal equipment and amenities.

Setting up

Even if you are going to subcontract everything out and simply act as an enabler or catalyst who brings it all together by using the skills of others, you will still need somewhere to work with at least the bare minimum of resources to contact people and do your organizing efficiently. It is just conceivable that you could run a publishing operation with an address (which could be an accommodation address) and a mobile phone by outsourcing virtually every function except decision making. You could dictate your letters to a secretarial service, talk to authors by phone, post manuscripts to a typesetter and the corrected text to a specialist printer as camera ready copy (CRC) or on disk, deal with the cover designer by phone and post, have the printer send the books to the distributor with whom you have made appropriate arrangements, telephone the PR and advertising agencies to whom you have given the job of promoting the book and simply bank the money and pay the bills. You *could*, but it is unlikely and certainly not to be recommended as a sensible model.

Depending on the scale of your operations at the beginning of your new publishing career, you will need either a small office or a desk in the corner of a room at home. I recommend the latter rather than taking on the expense of costly premises, as a year's rent of even the most modest office would pay for the print run of a book or a good promotional and advertising campaign for another. Think carefully about presentation and image when you make these decisions, for while it is not necessary at this stage for your publishing business to have its own office (you can meet clients or authors at a smart local hotel over a light lunch or a drink, or make sure that your meetings take place on their territory – for *their* convenience, of course!) it is important that the perception of your business on paper is sufficiently businesslike. So, if you live at 'The Laurels', 29 Laburnum Avenue, it may be preferable to use an accommodation address which gives a more businesslike impression. It might also help to utilize a service, which will take phone calls for you, using your name when they answer the phone. This will give a better impression than either your children answering the phone to an important client when they come home from school or callers always getting an answering machine message which implies that you are never there. Of course, if you live in a street which sounds as if it might be as good a commercial address as any other, then you can simply use your street number address following your business name, while some people add the words 'Suite' or 'Unit' number to the address to reinforce this impression.

What you will need

Wherever you locate your business, you will need to provide yourself with the requisite 'tools of the trade'. As a minimum I would suggest you need:

- a desk and filing cabinet
- a telephone and answering machine (preferably one which incorporates a fax unit)
- a computer with internet access
- a 600dpi laser printer
- a good quality desktop publishing (DTP) program such as PageMaker, Windows Publisher, Express Publisher or Quark
- a good graphics program – particularly if you are planning to publish newsletters or other illustrated publications
- a database program to keep records and mailing lists
- a set of postal scales
- a stapler.

If you buy all this equipment new, it could be quite expensive. However, if some items are already owned or bought second-hand the costs can be reduced considerably. You can, of course, accumulate them over a period of time – many a successful newsletter has been launched from a kitchen or dining-room table using nothing more than a typewriter, scissors and paste.

Additional items you might want to consider as your business grows are:

- a photocopier
- a scanner
- a franking machine for convenience and image
- a comb-binding or hot-melt binding machine.

You will, of course, require paper, envelopes, files, packing materials and other items of stationery. Try to avoid buying these from your local high street stores as they are usually available more cheaply from large specialist national suppliers (see Useful Addresses at the end of this chapter).

What will you publish?

While it is important that you have an adequate set-up to accomplish your publishing objectives, a much more important question is what you are going to publish, and in what format.

You may already have a clear idea of what it is that you want to publish. If so, be prepared to subject this to rigorous analysis to see if the idea is viable and whether it is likely to be profitable. If you are unclear as to what you will be publishing, have a look at the lists below which attempt to categorize publishing projects in terms of either content or medium (see also the suggested publishing projects in Chapter 10):

Content (by no means exhaustive)

Advertising	Financial
Animals and Pets	Geography
The Arts	Guides
Autobiography	History
Biography	Home Interests (cookery,
Careers	gardening, etc.)
Children's Publications	'How to...' Books

Community/Social
Computers/Technology
Crafts and Hobbies
Directories
Educational
Fiction

Humour
Occult, Paranormal, etc.
Poetry
Psychology/Self Improvement
Travel

Media

Audio tapes
Books on CD
Copiable Books
Electronic Books on Disk
Electronic Books on the Internet
Hardback Books
Information Folders
Internet E-zines
Magazines
Manuals, Guides/Special Reports

Newsletters
Newspapers
Paperback Books
Part Works
Posters
Ring-bound Courses
Telephone Information
Videos
Web Pages

Your choice of what content to publish will depend either on your own interests and enthusiasms or on your assessment of what topics and areas are likely to bring success in your publishing venture – in crude terms, what will make money! You may, however, want to approach it from the other direction and decide what kind of medium you want to operate in, basing your judgement on which medium appeals to you or which you feel more proficient to tackle – or on your assessment of the future success of that particular medium. Thus, you may decide (wrongly in my view) that the book is dying and only electronic and web-based publishing media are the shape of the future for publishing, or that your resources are best used by focusing on 'on-demand publishing', where you produce single copies of a comb-bound or hot-melt bound photocopied text when you receive an order for it. This can enable you to publish a very wide range of specialist publications for which the demand is relatively small without tying up capital and space in stock.

Here is an interesting concept which I first heard at a publishing seminar: take 50,000 words of text – what can you do with it and how much can you charge for it?

■ In newspaper format you could charge, say 50 cents

- As a magazine you could charge between $1.95 and $3.50
- A paperback book would sell the same information for $5–$10
- In hardback the price would range between $12.50 and $20
- However, in typescript and bound in a cover as a special report you could sell it for anything up to $100 – sometimes more.

Why?

The answer has to do with perception. If you buy a book or magazine you know what that particular format usually costs – in other words, no matter how valuable the information it contains, you are buying it and seeing it as an artefact of which you know the approximate value. On the other hand, when you buy a typed report *what you are buying is the special information it contains* – you don't tend to draw comparisons with other publications which sell within a particular price range. The same would apply if you were to make the same 50,000 words available on a computer disk as software or an electronic book: despite the fact that it costs you around 30 cents to produce, including a label and folded paper cover, you can charge more for it than for any printed format – which would cost you considerably more to produce – and, in most cases, you would have to produce and store more of them and tie up capital in the process.

Add to the above insight the corollary that price is (to most people) an indicator of inherent value rather than the result of an arbitrary decision of the producer, and you get the interesting proposition that the higher your price the greater the likely uptake in terms of sales. As one astute business adviser commented, firms rarely go out of business by charging too much, but many go broke from charging too little.

Choosing your project

So, what would you rather do – produce 1,000 copies of a 500-page specialist directory which has cost you $10,000 to print and that you sell at $60 and may only sell 250 copies, or produce an information product on computer disk which costs you 30 cents a copy beyond the authoring and origination costs and sells at $30? If you sell 250 of the first, you stand to make a gross profit of $5,000 less the cost of borrowing the capital to print and the warehousing and handling costs, not to mention the huge postage costs. With the second project you stand to make a profit on the very first sale and a potential gross profit of $7,425 from selling the same number of copies – with no capital tied up, no warehousing cost and minimal post and packing costs.

Don't, however, get carried away by your own enthusiasms into producing something with a content that excites you and in a form that suits you *without first thinking about who the product is aimed at*. Is there an audience that shares your excitement about the subject matter sufficiently to buy enough copies to make the project profitable? Is the price right – and is it produced in a medium appropriate to the potential buyers? It's no good producing an electronic book about how best to buy a computer for first-time buyers – at that stage they will not have the tools to read your publication! Nor can you sell a guide to escaping poverty if the medium is an expensive, glossy, full-colour book.

These are just some of the issues you need to think about before getting started on your first project. Clearly, if you are in love with a medium you have to choose projects that are appropriate to the medium, with content that is attractive to other people who are into that particular medium too. So you either have to choose the medium you want to work in and then focus your content on the concerns and interests of users of that medium, or you focus on the needs that readers and buyers have and then choose an appropriate medium in which to present that information.

Thinking it through

Clear-headed thinking is one of the most important business attributes to cultivate. Inspiration and enthusiasm are all very well, but they must be accompanied by careful and realistic analysis and the courage to say a firm 'no' to otherwise exciting and satisfying projects that do not make good business sense.

Here are some questions that may be helpful to ask yourself when thinking through a decision on whether or not to proceed with a particular publishing project:

- What are my reasons for wanting to publish this?
- What potential audience have I identified?
- Is this a product that is needed?
- Is this a product that is *wanted?* (Different question)

- Can I reach the potential buyers easily?
- Are there competing products already on the market?
- Why will my product be different from the competition?
- What is the appropriate medium for this product?
- What price range would be acceptable in the marketplace?
- Have I the capacity and ability to produce this product?
- Can I produce this product at a reasonable price?
- What are the profit margins likely to be?
- How will I sell the product? By mail order? On the internet? Through the book trade?
- Will the product have a long shelf-life or will it date quickly?
- Do I need to buy in additional (expensive) expertise to produce this product?
- Will the media be interested in this product?
- How well does this project fit into my overall publishing strategy?

As a starting exercise, think about a publishing project you would like to attempt, draft out the basic idea in a few short sentences and then write down your answers to the above questions in relation to this idea. At the end of the process you should have a pretty good idea whether or not you have a viable publishing project. Open a file for it and subject it to further analysis as you read through the further sections of this book – and then, get started!

Useful addresses

Stationery suppliers

Neat Ideas Ltd, Sandall Stones Road, Kirk Sandall, Doncaster DN3 1QU. Tel: 0800 500 192. Fax: 0800 600 192.

Viking Direct, Bursom Industrial Park, Tollwell Road, Leicester LE4 1BR. Tel: 0800 424 444. Fax: 0800 622 211.

Staples, Westfields, London Road, High Wycombe, Buckinghamshire, HP11 1HA. Tel: 0800 14 14 14. Fax: 0800 14 15 16. (See local trade directory for your nearest Staples superstore.)

Brewers of Helston Ltd, Water-Ma-Trout Industrial Estate, Helston, Cornwall, TR13 0LW. Tel: 01326 563424. Fax: 01326 563606.

COSTS Consortium Ltd, 64 Albion Court, Attleborough Road, Nuneaton, Warwickshire CV11 4JJ. Tel: 02476 37 37 38. Fax: 02476 37 36 46.

Note: Readers in countries other than the UK should consult the appropriate trade and business directories.

4 | WRITING AND EDITING

Whatever publishers may think, there is little doubt that the most important person in the process of publishing books and other information products is the writer. Without the writer there would be no words on the printed page (or recorded on the audio tape or acted out on the video or CD), no ideas and explanations to help and advise the reader and no concept on which a book or any other published item could be based. The writer is the one who conceives the project, the parent who brings it into the world and the nursemaid who nurtures it to maturity until it can stand in the world on its own. Without the writer, there would be nothing.

Of course, the publisher has a role to play too, for writers are notoriously unworldly, unbusinesslike and invariably unable or unwilling to push into the limelight and sell themselves and their wares. The publisher's job is to take the writer's creative output and package it in a format that will enable it to thrive in the marketplace and spread its message to readers across the country – or across the world. Without the publisher, the writer would perish, his words unseen, his ideas stillborn, his pockets empty. Writer and publisher need each other and, together, they bring wisdom and entertainment to the world through the printed page, the recorded tape or the digitized disk.

What is interesting in this partnership, however, is the imbalance of power and the differing financial rewards experienced in this symbiotic process. While publishers at the start of their careers will earn salaries which are far from princely, they will eventually climb the career ladder to earn reasonably comfortable salaries. By contrast, it is thought that the vast majority of writers earn less than the national minimum wage, with only one in seven being able to live on their earnings as writers.

Add to those dismal figures the fact that a great many more writers find it difficult to get their books published at all, while others find their books going out of print to make room in publishers' lists for new and potentially more profitable books, and the argument for the writer to become his or her own publisher sounds increasingly sensible.

The logic of this situation has led to a proliferation of alternatives to the traditional publishing route for writers. These include the submission of manuscripts or book ideas to more than one publisher at a time because it takes so long, in general, for publishers to make a decision (or sometimes even to give the courtesy of a reply) that by the time a book has been offered to and rejected for various reasons by several publishers it may well be no longer publishable – particularly if the subject matter is topical or cutting edge.

Vanity publishing has long fed on the difficulties of authors seeking publication and many innocent writers have spent thousands of pounds to have such firms 'publish' their books, where 'publish' simply means to produce a few copies, bind some for showing to the naïve author and do little or nothing to sell copies either to the trade or the public. Other services have tried to plug that gap by offering a more honest book production service for self-publishers who then have the responsibility for selling the 500, 1,000 or 1,500 (or more) copies, with little idea of just how difficult (indeed, in most cases, almost impossible) that is – which is why we have publishers, as well as writers.

There is, however, a case to be made for self-publishing and for some writers to become publishers in some of the ways we advocate within these pages. To put this into some kind of perspective, consider that established writer Mel Lewis earned considerably more from his self-published 2,300 word report, *Men – How To Make Sex Last Longer* than he was paid by an established publisher for his 60,000 word hardback book, *How To Make Money From Antiques*. However, this route is usually entirely unsuitable for most writers of fiction or for non-fiction writers who would find it difficult to reach anything other than a specialist market.

Basic writing skills

Since the central focus of this book has more to do with taking up publishing as a business aiming to make money, writing skills are not taken for granted as they might be for self-publishing writers, though it is assumed that someone interested in publishing as a business has some familiarity with and competence in writing in general.

If you do not have a good command of language, including at least an instinctual grasp of grammar and spelling (or an awareness of your deficiencies and limitations in this sphere), then publishing is not likely to be the right business for you to become involved in. As an independent publisher, you will find it expensive to buy-in the language skills you need and your judgement of the quality of potential manuscripts for publication will be, at the very least, suspect.

Whether you intend to publish only your own work or the work of other writers, you will need to be comfortable with and competent at handling the written word. Artistic licence and experimental writing aside, you will need to know the basic rules of language: what makes a sentence; the agreement of subject and verb; the proper use of words; the ability to judge what is and what is not good writing; the logical ordering of thought and content in sentences, paragraphs and chapters; the proper use of figurative language; the ability to spot lazy, ineffective or self-indulgent writing; and, perhaps most important, the ability to help a writer improve his or her writing to an acceptable standard for publication.

This is not to say that the language of your publications needs to be academic or stuffy. Style has one function only beyond decoration and that is to communicate clearly and effectively with the readers. As Defoe defined it, good style is '… that in which a man speaking to five hundred people … should be understood by them all'. Good advice for any writer: how do you achieve it? Here are some guidelines.

Be simple. Be direct. Prefer short sentences to long sentences. Use the active, rather than the passive voice ('fix the round piece to the flat piece with a screw' rather than 'the round piece is then fitted to the flat piece with a screw'). Be conversational (without being too sloppy). Think of a person who is characteristic of the people you are writing for and write as if you were explaining it to him or her. Avoid exclamation marks as far as possible. Use illustrations or stories that explain or illuminate a point. Make it relevant to the reader. Address his or her interests and concerns. Think like a salesman – attract attention, catch the readers' interest, rouse their emotions and involve them and propel them into action. Make it fun. Leave them gasping for more.

What an editor does

As an editor, your job is to manage the writer and the writing project so that on completion it is the best and most effective publication it can be. First, you have to find good writers (if you are not publishing your own material) and determine if what they have to offer is the kind of thing you want to publish, or if they are capable of working to your brief to produce exactly what you are aiming to produce and sell. You will then have to work closely with the writer to help them to achieve this effectively and within the time scale you have set.

As editor of a newsletter or special interest magazine you will carry the overall responsibility for the content of the publication, the selection of articles, features and fillers and for the overall tone and direction. You may find yourself having to correct and sometimes rewrite the material submitted by your contributors. This is part of the job as an editor of a periodical, but courtesy demands that when you feel you have to do a substantial rewrite you should do it with the agreement and after consultation with the writer – otherwise reject the piece and replace it with something else.

Some editorial principles

Since you are likely to be both publisher and editor (functions which are separated in larger publishing firms) some of the comments in this section will apply to the publishing side of things as much as to the editorial function. As a broad generalization, the editor is the person who deals directly with the author and the content and progress of the manuscript, turning it into a publishable proposition, while the publisher is, if you like, the overall manager of the publication process, taking a wider view that will include decisions about the print run, the sales and publicity and other aspects of the business of bringing books and other products to the market.

Saying 'no'

One of the first lessons the tyro editor or publisher needs to learn is how to say 'no'. You need to say 'no' to excellent products that do not fit into your publishing plan or area of interest. It can be very tempting to come across something you think is marvellous, but which you are not really in a position to publish or market alongside your other titles. Learn to say 'no' in an encouraging way and direct the author to a more suitable publisher if you can: it will be best for the author and certainly best for you. I still have copies of a book of short stories I published quite a few years ago because I was teaching creative writing and felt that there were too few outlets for many of the good stories my students were writing – a wrong decision for a mail order publisher of small business material as I didn't have the resources to market the book effectively. Publishing that book, simultaneously in hardback and paperback, was an indulgence, and one that I paid for dearly. Nevertheless I was pleased to have done it, even though it lost me money. I learnt a good lesson from the experience.

You need to learn to say 'no', too, to work, which simply isn't good enough – this can be harder than you think, especially if friends approach you with their pet projects. Say 'no' also to projects which are too ambitious in scale or scope for you to handle as a small (and, I presume, financially limited) publisher.

What do you want to publish?

As an editor you need to develop clear ideas of what, exactly, it is you want to publish, so that you can recognize it when it comes your way or an author makes a proposal. Knowing what you want to publish is essential if you are to give explicit briefs to authors. I publish a ring-bound writing course, *Earn £180 a Day Writing* and recognized that I needed to have other writing products to sell to my growing list of buyers. I commissioned another writer to produce a similar course on a specialist area, *Have Pen, Will Travel ... How To Make Money From Travel Writing* and, with the emphasis of my course being on how to market writing effectively, was able to brief my author to give the same kind of emphasis to her course, which will, therefore, include sections on free holidays and other perks, how much travel editors pay, negotiating fees, earning extra from photographs, selling ideas more than once, a quick and easy way to earn money from travel tips and so on. Those people who have enjoyed and benefited from my course on feature writing are likely to look favourably at extending their range by buying the new course on travel writing. What will they buy next? As an editor and publisher, I am now looking for the next writing product to offer to my list – indeed, a range of products, so that I can continue to offer my customers more of what they want while building a more profitable publishing business in the process.

Agreeing terms and content

You will also, as an editor, be responsible for agreeing a contract with your authors and, in an independent business, making sure that they are paid according to the terms of the contract and that they deliver the product that they are contracted to produce. As an editor you will need to develop a good working relationship with your authors, making sure that they produce what you want in the style and to the length you want, yet with the minimum of interference. Editors should encourage and motivate authors, yet must be prepared to step in with guidance and help when an author is floundering or not producing work to the standard required.

Sub-editing

Having worked with the author to produce a publishable manuscript written at the right level and in the appropriate style for the intended audience or market, the editor-publisher now has to put on another hat – that of the sub-editor. Sub-editing is concerned with the process of going over the text word by word, sentence by sentence and paragraph by paragraph to make sure that it is grammatically and factually correct, that the language usage fits the publisher's house style and preferred conventions, to smooth out any rough edges in the author's style and expression and generally to tidy up the micro-aspects of the work so that it is as perfect as humanly possible.

If you are doing this aspect of the publishing process yourself I recommend that you have, at least, a good dictionary. Whatever you do, don't rely on a computer spellchecker, which should be used only as a starting point or a failsafe. It is also advisable to have a guide to the use of the English language, a good dictionary of quotations (most popular sayings and quotations are often mis-remembered), and a dictionary for Writers and Editors is an absolute *must*.

Some examination boards produce excellent study courses which will enable you to become as good as any professional editor. You might also find it useful to contact the Society of Editors and Proofreaders, which runs training sessions and publishes a newsletter to meet the needs of both beginners and more experienced editors. See Useful Addresses at the end of this chapter.

Finding writers

If you are going to develop a good range of products beyond the ones you want to put together yourself you will need to find suitable writers. How do you go about this? One way is to get yourself listed in some of the publishers' or writers' directories. Later, when you are more established, you may find yourself being approached to have an entry in some of the larger publishing directories. Such listings will bring you enquiries and some writers will find you from the listings and offer you their wares. When you have a couple of publications under your belt, consider joining the Independent Publishers Guild (see Useful Addresses at the end of this chapter).

Keep an eye on magazines and journals within your area of interest and contact any feature or article writers whose work appeals to you as the kind you want to publish, and enquire whether they would be interested in writing for you. If you want to be swamped with material, place a small classified advert in a writers' magazine, being very specific about the kind of work you want. Another avenue is to contact groups or societies focusing on your area of interest, expressing a desire to contact potential writers or contributors. *The Writers' and Artists' Year Book* lists a wide range of societies and specialist writers' groups which may also be a source for you to tap.

Writing it yourself

Most people who develop an interest in publishing are also interested in writing and, in many cases, the spur to become a publisher is to publish some work of their own about which they feel passionate or that they feel has commercial possibilities. These two things are not mutually exclusive and an overwhelming enthusiasm for some obscure subject often overcomes the inevitable difficulties and barriers that narrow specialisms encounter. However, beware of being driven by enthusiasms that are so obscure or limited in appeal that you commit yourself to a never-ending struggle to make your publishing enterprise a paying proposition.

On the other hand, some of the publishing media and methods now available as the result of new and readily available technologies mean that you can profitably publish 50 or 100 copies of your specialist work and still turn in a profit. We will look at some of those possibilities in Chapter 6.

Assuming that you have the knowledge or the information for the product you want to publish, writing it should be relatively straightforward. For those with little or no experience of writing for publication the following guidelines might prove helpful.

1   First think about the medium that is appropriate for your project. If the ideal medium is a video or audio tape, then you will have to think in a different way from the way you would work on something designed to be produced as a printed text. You may have to think about visual elements, dialogue, sound effects, location shots, tone of voice, actors or presenters. You will effectively be writing a radio or TV script and these have special techniques of their own which you should familiarize yourself with. Clearly there isn't space here to go into details about this specialized kind of writing, but you will find it useful to read one of the many available books on the subject. The only bit of advice I would give at this point is not to treat an audio tape or video tape presentation as if it were a written text. In other words, use the pictures to show something that is harder to convey through the written word – don't just have 'talking heads'. Likewise, if you are producing an audio tape, use the medium by introducing sounds, different voices and music to emphasize, dramatize and enhance your message.

2   Whatever medium your product will appear in, the first step is to brainstorm and write down every possible idea, topic or heading you can think of in relation to the subject matter of your project. Once you have reviewed these and decided what should be included and what left out, the next task is to put them into some kind of logical order, with major headings which will become your chapter titles and subheadings, grouping similar ideas together. These will become the various sections of your chapter and the topics themselves, again arranged in a logical sequence, will form the text for that section. Having drawn up that structure neatly, you have the skeletal framework which simply needs to be fleshed out as you write it section by section, chapter by chapter.

3 Depending on the kind of product you envisage, you may want to include additional elements such as questions to be thought about by the reader, exercises to be completed, illustrations, diagrams or charts, or sidebars – those little boxes that sit within or at the side of the main text summarizing some important aspects of the subject, side issues or additional text such as case studies or other illustrative material that might hold up the flow of the main text.

4 Think carefully about the intended audience and market for the product. Are they specialist readers with a high level of education or are they ordinary people who may not be frequent or regular readers? Who they are will determine whether you adopt a careful, traditionally literate approach (as I hope this book does) or a more chatty, conversational style in which the niceties of grammar and expression are relaxed so as to appear more like a conversation with a friend. Decide too, whether the need is for straightforward no-nonsense information imparted as quickly, simply and efficiently as possible, or whether a more discursive style is appropriate to the readership you aim to serve.

5 However good your writing skills or your grasp of English or your spelling, get someone else to read your finished text before committing to print. No matter how competent you are, you can very rarely see all of your own mistakes. This is no reflection on your skills or your conscientiousness, but simply a result of how our reading process works. When we are fluent readers we no longer read word by word like primary school children, but by rapidly scanning text, taking in the general message and galloping forward to get the sense of the whole thing – which we do remarkably well. The trouble is that because we are so skilled at reading between the lines, filling in the gaps and guessing the meaning from the general context, our eyes fly over the words and can easily miss words repeated twice, used wrongly or other small errors that have crept in. Someone else, reading without our familiarity with the text, will pick up these things because they are reading more slowly and critically and can't anticipate what is coming in the same way that we can.

6 If you are more of a 'practical ideas' person with some valuable information to impart, you may find an audio tape presentation more natural and easier to handle. If, however, you think that the written format is preferable, then you could dictate your script and let a good secretarial agency type it up, with specific instructions to tidy up the grammar and expression. Another approach is to ask a writer to work on your rough draft or to act as a ghost writer for your project.

7 Take a tip from an ex-salesman and write from a 'you' perspective rather than a 'me' perspective. Whose concerns would you rather talk about – yours or somebody else's? Precisely. And that is why there is so much non-communication in all walks of life: people are interested in their *own* lives and their *own* agenda, not yours, so use this in your writing. Address the reader's concerns and focus on his or her interests – then you will be interesting to them and they will pay attention. Talk solely about *your* experience and *your* agenda and they will stop being interested and turn on the TV instead.

8 Make sure that your books, chapters and sections start and end with a bang. Make tantalizing promises to the reader – promises that you go on to fulfil in the words, chapter or paragraph that follows. That's not difficult. Here is how to do it …

9 Transfer the first line of your paragraphs, chapters or sections to the end of the previous one. If they are strong on promise, then they will pull the reader smoothly into the next part, eager to read the answer. Just study the end of every episode of your favourite soap and you will get the idea.

10 Never forget Rudyard Kipling's six little helpers:

> I keep six honest serving men
> (They taught me all I knew);
> Their names are What and Why and When
> And How and Where and Who.

Make sure that you cover the subject thoroughly, giving all the information that the reader will require – the what and the why, the when and the how, the where and the who. Cover everything.

Write the flyer first

This advice flies in the face of customary practice. Most business people make or procure their product first, *then* write the sales material after they have studied the features and benefits of the product. But there is sense in this reversal. What it means is that before you begin to produce a publication or information product you focus on what it is that the customer will ideally want to buy.

So, what you are writing is a flyer or brochure for an ideal or mythical product: the book which tells them all they need to know, the video tape that shows them just how to do it, the audio tape that reveals all the secrets of the subject they have always wanted to know.

In effect, writing the sales literature for this ideal product tells you the characteristics that your product ought to have, and so gives you a blueprint to work to. Your flyer or brochure is *the promise that your product or publication has to fulfil.* All you have to do now is to write it.

Useful addresses

A useful source of information and guidance for the author considering self-publishing is the Author-Publisher Network, SKS, St Aldhelm, 20 Paul Street, Frome, Somerset BA11 1DZ. This is an organization which was founded by John Dawes as a spin-off from a Society of Authors' specialist group and is a non-profit, self-publishers self-help organization which runs courses and seminars and publishes a newsletter *Write to Publish.*

Society of Editors and Proofreaders, Mermaid House, 1 Mermaid Court, London SE1 1HR. Tel: 0207 403 5141.

Independent Publishers Guild, 4 Middle Street, Great Gransden, Sandy, Bedfordshire SG19 3AD. Tel. (01767) 677753. The IPG publishes a membership list which describes the particular publishing interests of their members and the Secretary often makes available details of manuscripts from writers looking for a publisher.

Note: Readers in countries other than the UK will probably find equivalent organizations which they can contact for assistance.

5 | DESIGNING YOUR PRODUCT

There is a book that could be written about design in publishing. It would be a large undertaking, and not one that I am competent to write, as I am a writer and therefore word-based, working largely with the left-hand side of the brain which is predominantly logical, concerned with order, sense, clarity and fact. This means that what I have to say about design will be based on considerations of clarity, order and the importance of common sense and good communication rather than on creative and exciting visual qualities which are the domain of the right-hand or creative side of the brain. Which brings me to the question, what is good design?

You may think that I have disqualified myself above from commenting on the qualities of good design and you may be right. Nonetheless there are aspects of design that I consider to be of predominant importance over and above the creative side when creating an information product. I would argue (as you might expect from a writer) that the meaning, that is, the word content, of any publication (with the exception of an art-based or other visual product) has to be more important than how attractively it is packaged. That is not to say that those aspects of design – making the product attractive, easier on the eye, stimulating and therefore saleable – are not important. They are, but what is more important is that the ideas that the product is designed to impart are clearly conveyed to the reader, listener or viewer and that the design facilitates that objective rather than getting in the way.

Why good design matters

Good design will enhance the objective of the product, make it clear and easy for the reader to access and will present it in an attractive enough way for the reader to pick it up, buy it, use it and enjoy it. Poor design will make the publication (of whatever kind) dull in appearance, old-fashioned, or so 'way out' that it will dissuade potential readers from buying and benefiting from it. Poor design will also elevate attractiveness above function, for example presenting large blocks of print reversed out in small print on a black background, making it difficult to read.

It should be obvious, despite my emphasis on the written content of the published product, that good design matters. It matters because each publication or other information product you send out into the world not only has a job to do for the recipient, but it also does an important job for you. It represents you and what you stand for – either badly or to your credit – to your customers and prospective customers and may be a determining factor in your commercial success as well as in the reputation you end up with. Believe me, a poor reputation will stick, while a good reputation is worth a great deal more than you will ever save by producing poorly designed products: first impressions do count. If your products are good, then they also deserve to be well-designed.

Some basic design principles

Perhaps the most important principle is that good design is functional, that is, it should enhance the message or meet its purpose – a leaflet or card that will not easily fit into a standard-sized envelope, for example, is a design that will incur unnecessary expense, and a book that is not a standard size and does not sit easily on the shelves of either booksellers or book buyers will be very much more expensive to produce. A newsletter, sold by subscription, does not need the same kind of 'buyer appeal' gracing its front cover, as it will be bought sight-unseen for the content as described in a leaflet, brochure or advertisement where the design may be more significant. Attractiveness or good looks are, or should be, a by-product of this process rather than an end in itself or a cosmetic add-on. Design which is self-indulgent and pursued for its own end is poor design and should have no place in your publications.

Design should also be appropriate to the medium, to the message and to the audience. 'Bitty' magazine layouts are inappropriate for a book publication, as large blocks of unbroken text are inappropriate for a newsletter or magazine. Illustrations or graphics should be there because they perform a function – to illustrate a point, to add humour, to break up large indigestible chunks of text or to add information to the text. The print should be large enough to avoid eyestrain. How far is the design restrained by the purpose of the overall communication? Is full colour necessary? What are the cost restraints? What kind of illustrative material – photographs, cartoons, line and wash drawings, charts, etc. – are best suited to the work?

Good design follows the KISS principle – a salesman's mnemonic that translates as 'Keep It Simple, Stupid!' or, in a slightly more polite version, 'Keep It Short and Simple'. In other words, use as little design and embellishment as will do the job and no more. Cut away that which is unnecessary and do not let design run away with the project, turning it into a work of art rather than an information product.

There are a number of disparate elements to be considered when designing any information product. Here, we consider each aspect briefly at a very fundamental level.

Cover design

The cover of any information product needs to be given some thought. Whether it is a book, a magazine, newsletter, audio tape or CD cover it will be the first thing that any purchaser, reader, listener or viewer will see. Their initial reaction to your product will depend on that cover. It may be one of disappointment, indifference or sheer pleasure. Aim for the last, for even if the item has been bought unseen through a mail shot or newspaper advert the reader will still have expectations that will either be fulfilled or disappointed when they unwrap the package or tear open the envelope. As we know, first impressions are important.

While you need not feel it necessity to compete directly with the multi-colour productions of major publishing houses, your product's initial appearance (and, indeed, its whole design) will be compared with those more lavish items. Hence the insistence that the design element of your products is important given that you have to make your impact with minimal resources.

A simple but effective design in two colours on a plain white background can be both elegant and sophisticated and much can be achieved with a combination of imagination and restraint. For some products, such as an A4 manual or guide on some specialist subject sold by mail order, a plain cover with a simple lettered title can be sufficient. Where possible, the addition of some kind of carefully chosen pictorial element can add immeasurably to the general effect. An old photograph of the village green surrounded by quaint thatched cottages might enhance your guide to a historic village, while the cartoon on the cover of John Miles' *Design for Desktop Publishing* makes the undertaking seem less threatening, more achievable.

As with all design elements, it pays to keep your eyes open for examples of the kind of design that you find pleasing and effective and, while copying as such is an infringement of the designer's work, imitation, being the sincerest form of flattery, is not. Collect such examples and learn from them and your own design consciousness and ability will be improved.

Text and fonts

This is another field where whole tomes exist – and a minefield lies in wait for the amateur publisher. If desktop publishing has made it possible for anyone to become a publisher, it has also been responsible for unleashing much amateurish and bad design on an unsuspecting public. Just because your DTP system has anything from a dozen to hundreds of fonts there is no reason to use most of them in one document or publication.

There is a great deal to learn about typography and most of us will never get beyond the basics. What are these basics that you need to know?

Fonts

Fonts come in two basic formats, serif and sans serif. Serif typefaces are those traditional looking ones which have the little 'feet' and fiddly bits on the end, while sans serif are *sans* (without) these embellishments. You might decide that serif typefaces look a bit old-fashioned for your style of publication and decide that a nice clean modern typeface like continuum light will make it stand out. This may be so, but the readers will find it difficult to read, as with most sans serif typefaces, which are best reserved for titles, headers, sub-headings or short pieces of text on cards and other short or ephemeral publications. As you will find through experience, serif typefaces such as Times New Roman are designed for ease of reading and should be the choice for most lengthy texts.

Type size

Type size is usually given in 'points', a term that comes from the old metal type system that has largely been supplanted by computer generated type.

Most books will be printed in serif type with a point size of anything between 10 to 12 point, though some books attempt to save space and paper (and, presumably costs) by setting in small type at the expense of their readers' eyestrain, while books for people with visual impairments are usually set in large type of 18 points or more.

Spacing

Since the space between the words and lines of print significantly affect readability, some study beyond the scope of this book should alert you to both the problems of poorly chosen typefaces and poor spacing, as well as to how to enhance your text so that it is both pleasing to look at and easy to read. A broad rule of thumb is that the spaces between words must be greater than the spaces between the characters that make up the words, and the space between lines of type should be larger than that between the words. This crude guidance will ensure that the words stand out individually without running into each other and that the eye is led instinctively along each line of print without confusion.

Line of type

Another rule is that there exists a relationship between type size and the width of the line of type. A small typeface across an A4 sheet will be very much more difficult to follow with the eye than one where the larger size is proportionate to the page width. If circumstances or choice dictate the use of a small type size, then it should be printed on a smaller size page, on a smaller part of the page leaving white space, or in columns to increase readability. When using columns, the number of columns on the page and the size of the typeface should be related: a number of narrow columns should be set in a correspondingly smaller typeface while a larger typeface is more appropriate for a two-column layout.

In short, use your eyes and exercise your common sense when making decisions about typeface styles, point size and the size and layout of the page on which your text will appear.

Layout

The layout of your page should enhance your text in terms of both readability and attractiveness. The factor of readability has already been amply stressed, but the general appearance of a text will determine to some extent whether the reader will be attracted to read it in the first place. How many times have you picked up a book with an attractive cover and title and begun to skim through it, assessing its interest for you and closed it because the overall impression was of a dull layout or a text difficult to read because of the typeface chosen or the claustrophobic effect of a point size too small, or one whose large size suggests a book suitable for a ten-year-old?

Margins

As with all good design, layout should follow function. Note first that left- and right-hand pages are different, usually with a wider margin on the inside or spine edge. This has a functional purpose in that it avoids text becoming difficult to read because it is falling out of sight into the curve of the spine. Some modern books have large outside margins (which have no intrinsic purpose), with the blocks of text so close to the spine that reading them is often a near impossibility. This is design for appearance, design without thought.

Headers and footers

Give some thought to headers and footers. The header text running across the top of the pages usually consists of the book's title (shortened if necessary) with chapter titles sometimes appearing on the right-hand header. Page numbers are often put at the foot of the page (footer), leaving the header for titles, but can be put in the header with the title information.

You will also need to decide whether to put any footnotes at the bottom of the relevant pages or numbered at the end of the chapter or book, with the corresponding number in the text beside the item they refer to. Some books get round that problem by using a magazine device – the sidebar. This is a box set to the side of the text (or sometimes in a box in the middle of the text) with additional information that can be glanced at at a convenient pausing point in reading.

Magazines and newsletters

While books and similar publications share many of the same ground rules, newsletters and magazines have their own conventions.

Newsletters

Newsletters, being more soberly informative in purpose, do not need to be all-singing, all-dancing affairs in design terms. The aim here should be to have a look that echoes the style of the subject matter, so a newsletter about cottage gardening or real ale might tend towards a deliberately old-fashioned style, evoking nostalgia for the past, while a business newsletter will want to look crisp and modern, reflecting the up-to-date content it has to offer.

Newsletters will tend to have an almost identical look issue by issue, unlike magazines, which strive for the impact of variety and difference in each issue while still remaining identifiable. Often the editorial will appear on the front page instead of having a magazine-style cover and the text within will invariably be set in two or three columns, three being the more common. Articles and features will usually follow on in a straightforward sequence and sidebars will often be used to give hard information like prices, examples or figures. Colour will usually be restricted to one additional colour to the basic text (black for preference) and the paper is often coloured rather than white, with pastel shades such as buff or yellow being preferred.

Magazines

Magazine design is a much more complex matter, having much more illustrative content and with the graphic element considered as important in the overall appearance as the text. Magazines, like newspapers and newsletters, are set in columns, often using a grid system, with the column sizes being related to the need to fit in advertising of set dimensions. Of course, not every page needs to follow the same grid, and some pages can be allowed to be anarchic, with text and illustrations becoming the plaything of the graphic designer. This is fine, for magazines must have a sense of surprise, of individuality and style, unless they are of a more sober disposition where such eccentricity might offend the sensibilities of the readership.

Of all forms of publishing, magazine designing is the one where amateurism shows most. By following common-sense rules most people can produce a reasonable book or newsletter, particularly with the help of modern DTP programs with their template designs, but magazines demand a flair and complexity that is by and large beyond the capacity of the amateur publisher. Unless you have worked on a professionally produced magazine or are producing a low-key, plain style journal, I suggest you don't try to do it yourself.

Illustrations

Do you need to have illustrations in your publication? Again, my criterion is that of function. If you need them, what do you need them for? Simply to decorate or relieve the text? To illustrate something in the text? Because they are an intrinsic part of the book, such as photographs in a history of locomotives or diagrams to show how things are made or fit together? Illustrations certainly make a book or newsletter more attractive and that may be a sufficient justification in itself – and in magazines they are an absolute necessity. What is important is that you think about the need for illustrations and know why you are using them and what kind will serve your purpose best.

The quality of your illustrations is something else to consider. A crudely scanned-in photograph in a limited circulation hobby-type newsletter may be acceptable, but a hardback book will demand something of far higher quality. While you can sometimes get away with reproducing a well-defined photograph on the same paper as the text (if the quality of the paper is good) most other times you will need to think about including your photographs as a specially printed and inserted section of the book. Printers will be able to advise you what can be provided by the methods and equipment they use, so consult them at an early stage.

Other products

Increasingly the tyro publisher will be exploring publications in other kinds of media such as audio tape, video, CD-ROM, computer disk, computer files downloadable via the internet and so on. Many projects by new publishers will use mixed media. Design is equally important with these productions, although the design considerations and parameters may differ. While many proprietary packages and design programs will make the task of producing something reasonably professional in appearance and function, there will still be a lot of learning to do and the same need for a critical approach to questions of clarity and effectiveness in communication.

There are many fairly highly priced information products published on the internet and, while many of them are stunningly designed and presented, some are very poorly produced by amateurish means on the premise that what people are buying is good quality information. So you may pay $30 or more to download a video on internet marketing only to find that what you get is a talking head filmed in poor lighting and with even poorer sound equipment at a seminar in a hotel room with dreadful acoustics. While the information content is sound, it would be immeasurably enhanced by some planning, some specially shot and edited sequences and some production expertise. You can, I am sure, do better.

Don't forget

There are a number of technical matters that also have to be thought about at the planning and design stage of most paper-based products, like ISBNs, ISSNs and Bar Codes. The first two are the International Standard Book Numbers and International Standard Serial Numbers assigned to books and magazines respectively and bar codes have become a virtual necessity for any publication to be sold via retail outlets. These are dealt with in the next chapter.

Hiring a designer

The question of hiring a designer for your publishing project is an important one which may have a long-term effect on your success as a publisher. Investment in thoughtful and attractive design at the outset will provide you with a product that at least looks as professional as you trust the content will be.

Can you go it alone and do your own design? That depends partly on your own skills and confidence and on the nature of your project. Clearly, with the templates and other aids available in DTP and other programs, anyone should be able to learn the basics fairly quickly and be able to produce creditable newsletters, booklets, books and other items. However, with something more complex (and even for some simpler projects) the input of a suitable graphic designer – that is, one with appropriate experience – can make an immeasurable difference to the quality of the publication. Once that design element is put in place it should be a relatively simple matter to continue to use and adapt it, with occasional input from the designer to tweak or extend it as necessary.

Finding the right designer is not difficult; finding one you can afford can be rather more difficult. Ask your contacts for recommendations. Look in your trade telephone directory for local design studios. Approach designers listed on the mastheads of publications you like and see if they do freelance work. Contact the local art college and see if they will assign your brief as a work assignment for a student.

Having found some possible designers, how do you choose who will be right for your project? Ask, first, for samples of their work so you can see if you like their style and thinking. Second, work out what it is you are looking for in broad terms, being prepared to be open to new ideas and suggestions from the designer. Decide, on meeting them, whether you think you can work together. Ask for references and talk to the referees to see if they had problems, if the designer met necessary deadlines and so on. Decide on what basis payment is to be made and whether you can afford it. Finally, draw up a brief specifying what you want, how you are to work together, cost, and how payment is to be made.

Remember, the bottom line is that it is *your* project, *you* are the publisher and *you* carry the responsibility of getting your publication looking the way you want it so that it will be the success you know it can be.

Recommended reading

Great Pages: a Common-sense Approach to Effective Desktop Design by Jan V White, Scrif Publishing, ISBN 1 878567 01 2, $12.95

Design for Desktop Publishing by John Miles, Gordon Fraser, ISBN 0 86092 096 8, £16.50

Outstanding Newsletter Designs by Polly Pattison, Mary Pretzer and Mark Beach, Coast to Coast Books Inc., 1115 SE Stephens Street, Portland, Oregon 97214, USA.

6 | MAKING THE PRODUCT

Old forms, new options

While publishing has moved a long way since Caxton brought moveable type to England and set up his press at Westminster in 1476, the publishing process has altered very little from the perception of the buyer of books, magazines and newspapers. In reality, there have been many changes behind the scenes as new technologies and processes have been discovered and applied to the business of making publishing faster, cheaper and better.

As in all other fields, that process of change and discovery is continuously developing and the pace of technologically driven change gets exponentially faster. Not only does this drive down cost, but it makes the processes that underpin publishing more accessible, making some kind of publishing possible for almost anyone with a basic understanding of the processes and access to the new technology either directly or through the many agencies that provide these services such as printers, copy shops, computer and typing bureaux, video hire companies, recording studios and so on.

Since the process of change is so swiftly moving, it is inevitable that by the time this book appears some aspects of this account of the production processes available to the tyro publisher will already be superseded by new advances in print or electronic media. However, the emergence of new developments or the updating of any of the technological processes currently in use will not invalidate the existing methods of production but rather offer additional options for the appropriate method of presenting publications. The clay tablets that were the original publishing method appeared some 6,000 years ago in Mesopotamia and this method can still be seen used as a form of publishing in the poems and other texts cast in clay pottery plaques and sold through gardening centres. Newspapers, which were launched in England with the *Weekly News* published by Nicholas Bourne and Thomas Archer in May 1662 (though there were a number of little news sheets in existence before that and a tradition that stretches back to early Roman newsletters of the fifth century BC), still thrive today. So it is a mistake to think that just because we live in the age of the internet with the prospect of more and more exciting possibilities ahead, that the old forms will die off and become unusable. There is still plenty of mileage in books, magazines, newspapers, newsletters and other traditional print media and there will continue to be for many years to come. This chapter will provide an introduction to the basics about producing those traditional publishing items as well as encompassing some of the growing means of publishing in the new media which became increasingly important in the twentieth century and will become more complex and varied in the twenty-first.

Books

The cost of book production, both hardback and paperback, has fallen dramatically as a result of advances in printing technology. The cost of originating the text has also dropped to potentially zero from traditional typesetting using lead lettering placed laboriously, if skilfully, by hand. First came photo-electronic typesetting machines of fearful expensiveness which worked like very complicated electric typewriters and were only available to the trade. Then came personal computers, those mysterious black boxes that at first seemed designed to do nothing that the ordinary person would find useful before developing into the familiar desk top wizards that almost everyone has today. I remember well the excitement generated at a small press exhibition where someone put on a demonstration of typesetting on a primitive 64k Commodore home computer. What a breakthrough that was – it was the beginning of desk top publishing, as it came to be called, and opened up the possibilities of much more professional publications from small and home publishers.

Software

Using widely available software it is now possible for an author to typeset his or her own book with the program providing page formats, headings and sub-headings, text styles and most of the aspects of typesetting that book readers are familiar with. Of course there are limitations imposed by lack of expertise and knowledge, but it is certainly possible to produce camera-ready copy straight from a laser printer from which a book printer can put together page layouts and print a serviceable and presentable book.

There are many such text production programs available, among which the most often used by professionals are Pagemaker, Ventura and Quark-XPress. Other well-known packages are Windows® Publisher and Serif Page Plus. There are other, less well-known programs such as the one I have used for years, 1st Press, the disadvantage of which is that the files cannot be read by or transferred to other programs. At the other end of the scale QuarkXPress, now the industry standard for mainstream publishing, is very sophisticated and not the easiest program to learn or work with. Although I have not yet used it, Windows® Publisher seems to have become the standard for non-mainstream or home publishing and has the advantage of being about a sixth of the cost of Pagemaker. Bear in mind, too, that today's sophisticated word processing programs such as Word 6 for Windows® can do a great many of the things for which DTP programs are bought. If your project is simple and less sophisticated than a traditional book, then a good word processing package or one of the cheaper DTP programs should be adequate.

Print runs

Changes in technology at the printing end of book production have made it possible to produce short runs of both paperback and hardback books at reasonable cost, with runs of 1–10 copies feasible (if expensive) and runs of 500–1,000 being reasonably economical. Of course, the cost per copy comes down significantly when print runs are increased to, say 3,000 or 5,000 copies but, apart from the capital that has to be tied up in stock at this level, there remains the question of whether you can sell such quantities. It makes little sense to pay only £3 per copy for your 3,000 copies when you end up with 1,700 stacked up in the back bedroom or garage and unsaleable. Better to print 1,000 at £4 a copy and order a reprint of 500 at £5 a copy. Work out the figures for yourself, but if the book were sold at £9.95 the gross profit in the first instance would be £3,935, while in the second you would make a gross profit of £6,435 and have only 200 unsold books to dispose of instead of 1,700. I know which scenario I'd rather choose.

Printers

In choosing a printer, don't simply contact your local general, all-purpose printer. They will almost certainly give you a price for your book and be quite happy to do it, but invariably the price will be high and they are unlikely to turn out such a good job as a specialist book printer who will have appropriate book-printing machinery using plates that will print anything from eight to 32 pages at a time.

Avoid those 'publishers' whose adverts are often seen inviting authors to submit books for publication. These 'vanity publishers' will charge exorbitant amounts to produce a few copies of a book and do virtually nothing to promote it. Do not even consider them to produce your book. What you need is a good short-run book printer working for the trade at reasonable prices.

If you feel nervous about dealing with a professional book printer you might be advised to work on your first project with a book packager who are also publishers. They will make a modest charge or profit from producing your book, working with one of the short-run printers and, while this will cost you a little more than going directly to the printer yourself, it will be well worth it in terms of what you will learn through their experience. You may, in fact, decide that you are happy to continue to sub-contract the actual production to such a firm, concentrating yourself on writing, getting authors and material and on the marketing and sales side. The details of a number of short-run book printers are given at the end of this chapter and you will be able to find more to widen your choice as your experience in publishing grows.

In planning your book and preparing it for the printer you will need to undertake the following:

1 Check the text, whether the author's or your own, for spelling, punctuation, stylistic deficiencies and matters of fact that need to be corrected.

2 Have the text typeset if necessary. If it comes on disk it can be imported into a DTP program and formatted to the text style and size chosen with headers, footers and page numbers as required.

3 Prepare and typeset the prelims, that is, the pages that precede the text which, in most cases, will be right-hand pages, blank on the reverse. You will normally require:

a) A half-title page carrying the title only (often dispensed with nowadays).

b) A blank page on the reverse of the half-title page.

c) A title page giving the title, any sub-title, the author and the publisher.

d) A page of bibliographical data on the reverse of the title page, giving: the name and address of the publisher in full; the copyright symbol against the name of the copyright owner (usually, but not always, the author) and followed by the date; the date of publication (if different); dates of reprints or new editions; the British Library Cataloguing in Publication data and International Standard Book Number (ISBN) which you will have obtained previously (see details below).

e) A Contents page.

f) A list of illustrations if required.

g) The Preface, which indicates the genesis of the book and may contain acknowledgements.

h) The Introduction, which explains the extent, scope and purpose of the book in terms of its subject matter.

4 Prepare any appendix that is needed which the author has not supplied, an index and, if necessary, a bibliography and a glossary of terms.

5 Have the book jacket designed and preferably presented as a colour separation. Printers can work from an unseparated design, but will charge for any further work they have to do on the originals before printing.

6 Liaise with your chosen printer over the way they prefer to receive illustrative matter and how it is to be processed and printed in the finished book.

7 Obtain an ISBN for your book from the Standard Book Numbering Agency (see Useful addresses at the end of this chapter).

8 Obtain a bar code to go on the back cover (many retailers insist on this for their electronic till systems which collect data and control stock, otherwise they won't consider buying your book). One firm which produces barcodes for books and magazines is Axis Multidata (see Useful addresses at the end of this chapter).

Hardback or paperback?

Which format should you choose, hardback or paperback? You may be desperate to see your name on a 'real' book – a hardback with a nice glossy jacket and your photo on the back but, putting vanity aside, ask yourself what is appropriate in terms of the audience and sales and profits. Publishing, after all, is a business and the point of a business is fundamentally to make profits. What you have to balance is the relative cost of each format against the profit potential, as well as the capital employed and the appropriateness of the format. If yours is a reference book and likely to be used a great deal then you may decide it has to be in hard covers, as the softback or paperback format is more ephemeral. What about the relative costs and profits?

If you can produce 1,000 copies of your book in paperback for, say £3.50 a copy, as opposed to 1,000 in hardback for £5.25, it is obvious that if you were to sell the total number of books produced you would make more profit from the hardback version. Look at the numbers: if you sold the paperback at £9.95 (a modest enough mark-up – most publishers will work on a selling price of three to five times the production cost) your profit on the 1,000 books would be £6,450. Alternatively, selling 1,000 hardback books at, say, £14.95 would produce a gross profit of £9,700. So, for an extra £1,750 – or £1.75 per copy – you would make an extra £3,250 gross profit without any extra marketing costs (though your post and packing or delivery costs will be greater due to the heavier weight of the hardback book).

Important considerations

Take this process a stage further and you will see that your profits on any project will depend, at least to some extent, on the publishing format you choose. If you were to take 50,000 words of information and put them in a newspaper format you could charge somewhere in the region of 30p–50p for it. Put the same text into magazine format with a glossy cover and the retail price would be around £1.50–£2.95. As a paperback you could set a price of £5–£10; in hardback, £10–£16. Put it in a ring binder and describe it as a study course and an acceptable price could be anything from £25–£120. However, if you produced it as an A4 typescript, put it in a plain binding and called it a special report you could charge virtually anything you like for it. Depending on the intrinsic value or specialist nature of the information, such reports can sell for up to £120 or even £300.

Read that paragraph again, because it could be the most valuable information about publishing you will ever come across. Why? Because it tells us that what is important in terms of what and how people buy is determined by their perception of what they are buying. We all know the approximate cost of a newspaper or magazine. We know the price range of books and what we are prepared to pay for them. We understand that a study course in a ring binder will cost more than a book because its size and presentation cause us to see it in a different light. When we buy a special report, guide or manual, we understand that what we are buying is the information it contains and that perception is quite different from our perception of the same process when it involves buying a book or newspaper. Moreover, the idea of exclusivity is involved in our purchase of either a study course or a special report, as these are rarely bought through a retail bookshop but sold by mail order.

From the publisher's perspective there are other advantages that make some formats more profitable than others. The cost/price ratio of study courses and special reports is highly favourable (the same is true of newsletters). The cost of producing a 140-page manual of the type described, using a laser printer and a hot-melt binding machine or similar, will be around £2.50 and to produce the same as a ring-bound study course can be as low as £3.50, yet the sale price of both can be between 10 and 20 times the production cost. Of even greater significance is the fact that very little stock needs to be carried, with reports or courses being printed up, bound and packaged for mailing as orders arrive. This is publishing on demand in a way that is not yet feasible for traditional books and magazines, despite advances in technology.

The same considerations apply to publications marketed as electronic books on floppy disk or CD which cost around 25p–50p to produce in the most unadorned form plus a few extra pence for labels and covers. Yet the price that the market will pay for these formats in specialist areas can be upwards of £15 – a profit margin of 2,900 per cent. And it gets better: an electronic book delivered over the web by e-mail or from a website by autoresponder costs nothing at all in terms of production and fulfilment – the publisher's ultimate dream!

Reports, guides and manuals

In the world of the small publisher, these terms are often interchangeable and can be anything from one or two pages up to 100 pages in length and may cost anything from zero to hundreds of pounds. They will generally be about fairly specialist areas, such as *How To Set Up Your Business As a Franchise* or *The Environmental Impact of Deforestation* or *A Guide to Building Your Own Computer*. Whatever the subject, they should be aimed at a particular segment of a specialist market rather than covering the sort of topics that can be found on any library or bookshop shelf. Your guide, report or manual should ideally be, information that is not readily available from other sources either because it is a minority or specialist interest or because it is a 'hot' topic that people want to know about fast like information on 'mad cow disease' or travel without petrol during a sudden crisis or shortage.

Reports and guides usually have minimal typesetting, being fundamentally a typescript within plain covers although, with the advent of computers and the variety of fonts and typefaces available, the presentation of such publications can be much improved. The actual pages can be output as CRC (camera ready copy) from computer using a laser or inkjet printer with these master copies being photocopied for the actual production run. It may even be economical to run sale copies straight off the laser printer as orders are received, though this can tie up your printer inordinately.

Binding

There are a number of ways in which such reports, guides or manuals may be bound. You can equip yourself with a long-arm stapler and use it to produce your reports as A5 booklets by reducing your A4 originals and printing them two-up and double-sided ready for folding and stapling into A5 format. Such reports, however, appear better presented in A4 format and your pages can be bound in several simple ways, the best of which demand the use of tabletop binding machines. Small, A5 reports can often be used as introductory items either at a low price or free to gain a customer. In the next chapter this approach to gaining customers will be looked at in detail.

Almost any local printer can print you a few hundred copies of such an A5 booklet, but you may do better by going to one of the printers who specialize in such work. See Useful addresses at the end of this chapter or consult your local trade telephone directory for details.

The simplest form of binding is, of course, to staple the pages of your report either at the top left-hand corner or with two or three staples down the left-hand side. This crude approach may be enhanced or replaced by putting a sliding plastic bar over the stapled left-hand edge and adding a simple cover sheet, or you can use the more sophisticated plastic clamp binders with a clear front and the capacity to hold up to 100 sheets of paper. None of these methods is acceptable for anything other than a cheaply priced report. For more substantial and higher priced publications you will need to use a binding machine.

Binding machines

The first of these binding mechanisms is the hot-melt machine in which the pages are inserted in a set of covers with ready-glued spine. When put in the machine the glue melts, binds the pages to the spine and you have a ready-to-post manual, guide or report.

The other, perhaps more familiar, form of binding machine is the spiral binder which has two operations: the first being a punch to make holes for the spiral wire or plastic comb binding to be inserted by the ingenuity of the machine in the second part of the process.

The third type of self-binding machine is the channel binder which is based on a metal channel in the spine that is made to grip the papers between the covers by the action of the machine. This form of binding can be taken apart up to three times for the insertion or removal of material.

All these binding machines can be obtained from office supplies companies. Some thermal binding machines are often offered free as long as you buy a sufficient quantity of binding covers.

While these methods put you in total control of the production process and allow you to produce single copies of any of your publications on demand, it does tend to turn you into a machine operator unless you have staff to do the work. It may pay to have pages bulk copied or even copied and bound by a printer offering this service, though it is best to shop around rather than use high street bureaux.

Newsletters and magazines

Newsletters

Perhaps the simplest form of publishing is producing a newsletter, thousands of which have been created by club secretaries, small businesses, hobby enthusiasts, school children, political parties and every conceivable kind of group you can imagine. At its most basic, all that is required is a piece of paper, some means of putting text and possibly illustrations on it – be that a typewriter, a computer and printer or even a pen in the hand of someone who can write or print legibly – plus some means of producing multiple copies. Newsletters used to be produced on ink duplicators after being typed on fragile stencils or on even more primitive spirit duplicators which could produce several colours at the same printing – even if the print tended to be faint, blotchy or otherwise imperfect.

Now it is the photocopier which serves as the printer for small-scale newsletters and some are even printed as required straight from the computer onto a laser printer, popped in an envelope and sent off to the new subscriber. This is certainly the route to follow when launching a new newsletter rather than getting hundreds of the first issue printed at considerable expense.

Apart from the sheer physical effort of producing hundreds of newsletters by hand, once numbers reach the hundreds, it becomes economic of time as well as cash, to have the newsletters printed by a professional printer on offset-litho or one of the new digital printing machines that have cut the cost of small-run printing.

Planning

In planning your newsletter you will need to know what size of paper your printer's machine uses. For a standard A4 size newsletter it will need to print on A3 paper, producing four pages of your newsletter on each sheet. This means that the number of pages your newsletter consists of will have to be divisible by four and if a larger machine is used, printing on A2 paper, then your newsletter will have to be 8, 16 or 24 pages (anything larger is veering towards becoming a magazine).

While many newsletters are printed on coloured paper, with buff or cream a favourite, there are advantages in sticking to plain white paper and introducing colour in your masthead. Black print on white paper is still the clearest and easiest to read and white paper is considerably cheaper than coloured stock. This is an important consideration when unit cost is an important component of profitability.

Consult your printer about how newsletter copy should be presented. Some will be happy simply to have the separate numbered sheets, but if your printer is printing on A3 sheets it is preferable for your own peace of mind to put the pages together in the right order. This will mean that any mistakes in pagination are more likely to be yours – at least it limits the possibilities for errors to occur.

To do this is quite easy.

1 Simply take the same number of A4 sheets of scrap or blank paper as your newsletter will be printed on, put them together and fold in half to make an A5 mock-up. So, if your newsletter has 12 pages you will have three folded sheets of A4, giving you a corresponding 12 pages of A5.

2 Number the mock-up pages from 1 to 12 (or according to the number of pages your newsletter has).

3 Open these sheets out flat so that the first page and the last page are facing up.

4 Take the first and last pages of the camera-ready pages for the newsletter and place them face up on the table so that they are in the same position as the two mock-up pages.

5 Turn these pages over, keeping them in the same order, and join them together down the seam with masking tape. (Tip: do this by using small pieces to first join them at the middle, top and bottom as this enables you to hold them still in position with one hand while sticking the pieces of tape with the other – then stick longer pieces in the remaining gaps.)

6 Put these joined pieces aside, face down, turn over the two mock-up pages to show the numbers on the reverse and repeat the process, putting that sheet aside and going onto the next and so on until the last two pages you stick together are the two middle pages.

Easy, wasn't it? (Well, it's easier to do than actually describe in words!)

Magazines

Magazines are a more daunting proposition for the small-scale publisher, for, as judged by the contents of the news-shelves, they are among the most complex in terms of colour, design and variety of content. However, the small-scale publisher is not likely to be in direct competition with the news-stand trade, as his or her magazine is probably aimed at a small specialist readership who will be reached by direct mail or advertising. A perfectly acceptable small magazine with a small circulation of between 1,000 and 5,000 can be produced to service such enthusiast groups printed on glossy paper mainly in black and white with the introduction of a second colour on some pages. The use of good layout and design will serve to mitigate the absence of full colour and good, well-chosen content with reader identification and participation can make such a magazine a runaway success in its own terms as a subscription-based magazine. You will see in the next chapter that distribution by subscription has much to commend it over the lottery and fierce competition of news-stand sales.

As with books, you will want to find a suitable printer who has experience of the kind of magazine production you have in mind. This is more likely to be a small printer dealing in relatively short-run magazine printing than the large national companies which produce the big glossies that you see in the newsagents. Check your local trade telephone directory for details.

Postcards, posters and other ephemera

It is easy to forget that publishing encompasses a wider range of items than books, magazines and similar products. Many publishers have started their publishing career by producing what are usually known as ephemera – postcards, posters, poem cards, single sheet guides, tourist trails, information cards and so on. These can be quite profitable, depending on the market demand and the accessibility of the market. Clearly a guide consisting of a single sheet of paper sold through retail outlets across a whole county is likely to cost more to promote and deliver than will emerge from the profits at the end of the year. However, a series of such guides sold through the same outlets may turn out to be quite profitable. The key here is high volume of low cost items as against the more secure profits from a lesser number of higher priced items.

Printers

As with book and magazine production, it is important to get the right printer, though in the case of the smaller items considered here this will be much easier. Be aware of one important thing: print costs are extremely variable in any field, so it is not only important to get the right printer – that is one who has the appropriate machinery and expertise for the job you are having printed – but to get a number of quotations from several printers. In the search for good, reliable and economic printers investigate both local printers (who are often surprisingly cheap) and national specialists. You can often find good printers from the adverts in printing magazines or the trade telephone directory. Also consider finding information from printing federations or associations.

Postcards and similar small items can often be produced economically by printing them four to a sheet of A4 card, especially if you are venturing into colour printing. This is an excellent way of publishing poetry as individual poems, as people will pay 20 or 25p for an attractive poem card that has cost only 2p to 4p to produce – you need large mark-ups on smaller items. With publications like postcards and posters (perhaps more than with books and other more extensive publications) you will need to give careful consideration to such issues as the quality and texture of the paper or card on which they are to be printed (weight, colour, glossy, heavy weave, hand-made and so on) and, in the case of high quality items, whether to use an older printing technology such as letterpress to get the kind of quality that only letterpress can give in some instances. Your printer will be able to give you much helpful advice here: listen and learn.

Design

Consider, too, using the services of a calligrapher for 'homespun' poetry posters and other suitable items. You will often find that by approaching adult education institutes in your area you can find a skilled teacher with good pupils who will be happy to undertake such work at reasonable rates to provide you with CRC suitable for taking straight to the printer of your choice.

Study courses and part-works

While it is unlikely that you will be able to compete with the big publishers of part-work courses which are seen from time to time on the news-stands (great art, military vehicles, gardening, etc.) in full colour, there is nevertheless a rich seam for the small publisher in both study courses and part-works. And, apart from the scale of their marketing, you can compete with the so-called correspondence colleges in providing good value study courses, especially in niche areas.

Study courses

Study courses are fundamentally of two kinds, the first being a comprehensive educational course without the interactive element of personal postal tuition and the second which adds that element. Both types can come in the form of either loose-leaf pages in a ring binder or as separate booklets. Where there is no interactive element the course is either sent out to the customer complete or on a monthly basis on the theory that it helps the reader to pace him- or herself. In the case of the tutored course the parts are usually sent out following the receipt of a completed assignment. The decision as to which format to use will be determined by a number of things, not least marketing considerations which are dealt with in the next chapter.

Presentation

The simplest and most economical way to produce a study course is to have the contents photocopied or printed in small quantities and to punch them with a four-hole punch and insert them into presentation ring binders. An A4 title page can be slipped into the plastic pocket at the front of the binder and you have a reasonably substantial and professional looking publication. Of course, if your budget runs to it you can have ring binders specially printed on the cover and spine for remarkably little and in reasonably small numbers. A company which can provide this service is ABC Graphics. See Useful addresses at the end of this chapter.

You may decide to use dividers to separate the parts of the course. If you buy the standard set of 12 numbered dividers you could plan your course to be exactly 12 modules. However, you can now buy special sets of dividers with clear tab labels onto which you can stick labels printed on your computer on clear stock.

Using the most basic method of a presentation ring binder with a self-printed insert on the front and photocopied pages, hand punched and inserted, a study course of this kind can be produced, packed and posted for as little as £7 and can be produced on demand as individual orders are received. This makes it an extremely easy publishing project to launch with virtually no capital, very little risk and potentially high profitability, as your selling price can be anything from £25 to £150 depending on the perceived value of the information it contains and the degree or otherwise of ongoing tuition supplied.

Distribution

If you are sending out the course in monthly parts or in response to the latest assignment submitted, you need only produce the parts as and when they are required. Assuming you have identified appropriate tutors to mark assignments (if you are not doing that yourself), you will need to devise a system to deliver the parts and marked assignments. One simple method is to supply a number of vouchers with each course corresponding to the number of tuition sessions allocated, each of them to be sent to the assigned tutor (at his or her home address) with the completed assignment. The tutor then sends the marked assignment to you to be returned with the next part of the course and includes the voucher for payment of the agreed tuition fee.

Part-works

What is the difference between a study course and a part-work? Not a lot, really, as they are much the same thing by different names though with a different emphasis. Study or correspondence courses tend to have some personal postal tuition through a series of marked assignments, while part-works stand alone as a series of lessons or information units for self-study without that tuition element. Some part-works are impressively designed and printed booklets, usually A4 in size, but others are photocopied sheets in a plastic folder, sometimes of extremely dubious value in terms of information and/or cost.

Clearly, to produce a course or part-work in the form of printed booklets involves a much greater expenditure of capital or, alternatively, a great deal more work producing them yourself using one of the simple home-binding methods covered earlier in the chapter. However, there is no doubt that a series of well-designed booklets or manuals is an impressive way to supply a specialist course and makes fulfilment and delivery easy – just pick the relevant booklets off the shelf, pop them in a bubble-wrap envelope and post them to clients once a month. Bear in mind, however, that information dates fairly rapidly and it is more difficult and expensive to update a course that is printed and bound than in loose leaf format printed as required from camera-ready copy.

Keeping that flexibility not only makes for an easier production process, but also provides the opportunity to upgrade the course and increase its perceived value by adding new information, supplements and other material so that the course grows in size, value and recognition. Think, too, of adding other elements such as an audio tape, video tape, computer software on disk or CD or any other item that makes it more comprehensive, more exciting and more satisfying to the buyer.

Another format for this type of publication is the study kit, a collection of documents, booklets, forms, examples, audio cassettes, etc., which come packaged in some kind of folder or case. You might, for example, have a study kit on growing miniature Bonsai trees which could contain a book or manual on the subject, packets of seeds for planting, some collapsible pots, tiny gardening tools, an illustrative chart of some kind and a video tape featuring an expert grower. A study kit of this kind can command a high price, though the production involves putting together products in different areas and is therefore more complex than some of the more traditional publishing projects.

Audio and video information products

Like the print media, audio and video production is easily accessible to everyone and, in the same way, this can open doors for easy entry into publishing in this field as well as opening the door to extremely poorly produced products. For the new entrant to the world of publishing the aim must be to strike a happy medium in the absence of access to state-of-the-art broadcast quality equipment and facilities so that what is produced is of an acceptable quality, reasonably attractively packaged and of good value in relation to the information covered and its presentation.

Why should you consider publishing in an audio or video format? There are a number of reasons that make such publications attractive. The first is the growth in interest in sound and television and its popularity as a medium. This has been enhanced by the corresponding drop in interest and ability in reading among substantial numbers of the population. Moreover, listening and seeing are both easier and more effective for absorbing new information, with the added advantage that audio cassette tapes are ideal for whiling away tedious car journeys and putting that time to better use as a learning experience.

In selecting subject material for an audio or video publication you should consider first and foremost its suitability for the medium. What are the advantages of putting this particular material in a sound or moving visual format? Does it require several 'voices'? Dramatic dialogue? Demonstration of a process that has to be seen to be understood? Would it be better on paper? In other words, there has to be a reason for the choice of format other than the fact that you like the medium. It may be that the consideration that leads you to choose the medium is that which we identified earlier, that listening to a tape or viewing a video is the preferred way of absorbing information. That's fine – as long as you are making a decision based on a rational analysis and not on a whim.

Audio tape production

Once you have decided on the subject matter the first requirement is to turn out a suitable script. This has to be written for voice rather than the literary page. In other words, its tone must be casual and conversational, talking to the listeners rather than lecturing them. Unless you have an attractive speaking voice (ask others, who will be tough critics, to tell you the truth) you will have to find someone with experience of speaking or reading to an audience to record the material for you – perhaps several voices. You may find someone by approaching the local drama school or college, or one of the lesser stars of your local radio station may do it for a modest fee.

Content

Your script will have to be timed accurately, including pauses, introductory music or sound effects. Remember to check the copyright position of any music you intend to use. There are a number of sources of copyright-free music and sounds specially produced for home movie makers and others which it may be advisable to use, or you may find a local musician who would be happy to play you some of his or her own compositions in return for a credit. Make sure that there is a natural break in the middle if you intend to carry over onto the second side of the tape.

The recording

Although you can record at reasonable quality with a decent home cassette recorder in a quiet room, you will get a much more professional sound quality by using a proper audio studio. You should be able to hire one by the hour in any reasonable sized town but you can cut costs by looking around for facilities at the media studies department of the local college, the local hospital radio station or by contacting a band or musician with their own recording facilities.

Your recording should be made on the highest quality tape and recording system within your reach, preferably on professional reel to reel equipment to provide a high quality master tape from which copies can be made by a professional cassette copying company. Good equipment will enable skilled editing to be done and for sound effects or music to be recorded on separate channels and blended together as required. If you have to record at home, make sure that you do so in a quiet room with plenty of soft surfaces to avoid echoes, close the curtains and cover hard table surfaces with blankets or tablecloths to absorb noise. A home produced tape will be inferior to one produced in a studio, but bear in mind that you are not producing for television and your tape, if done as carefully as possible, will be adequate to convey the information you are trying to get across in a way that will be reasonably acceptable to your listeners.

Duplicating the master tape

Once you have your master tape you need to turn your attention to the business of getting copies made in appropriate quantities. You could simply copy them on your home twin deck console, but the quality would not be very good. Professional copying services are available at an affordable cost and you will find them listed in specialist magazines devoted to music, home movie making, etc. Two that provide cassette duplication and associated services, including printing of labels and inserts are Downsoft Ltd and Fair View Music. See Useful addresses at the end of this chapter.

Video tape production

The first thing that you have to realize in considering publication in this medium is that while it is important to be as professional as possible and to produce the best video you can within the limits of the equipment and facilities you have access to, you will not be able to compete with professional film makers.

What you are engaged in is the dissemination of information, not the film business, and it is quite possible to produce a decent information video that will serve that purpose and satisfy the purchasers that they have got what they paid for.

The technology now available in contemporary digital video cameras, with built-in preview and editing facilities plus the added techniques available through specialized video editing computer programs, mean that you can produce technically competent films. The big question is whether you can actually produce an information video that is interesting.

The great majority of amateur video camera enthusiasts, like the generation before them who took home movies on 8mm or super-8 film, have simply no idea of narrative structure – indeed of structure of any kind – as those who have been forced to sit through miles of their friends' holiday movies can testify.

Nor are many of the existing instructional videos (with some notable exceptions, particularly in the field of keep fit) much better. Some are produced simply by setting up a video camera at some seminar or other, so all you get are 'talking heads' with the occasional cut away to the audience, usually with a desperate swinging and zooming as the inexpert camera operator tries to home-in on the person asking a question – which, of course, you can't hear, as the microphone on the camera is picking up all the background sound against which the mumble of the questioner cannot be heard. The platform speaker, who has the only personal microphone attached to the system, invariably answers the question without repeating it, so the viewer is left to try to figure out what the answer means and reconstruct the question from the answer.

Talking heads are boring, even when live. Research has established that the human attention span to a speaker is about 20 minutes, so an instructional video which consists of an inexpert performer stumbling through a presentation for 50 or 60 minutes is a poor medium of instruction.

Why video?

What video is good for, surprisingly, is showing things – particularly moving things. If you are going to present a talk, you might as well put it on audio tape. That means that the content of your message must be considered to see if video is the appropriate medium for publishing it. What will be gained by using video? What will you be able to show? Would some other medium be better suited to convey your message?

Once you have decided that there are good reasons for choosing video as the best medium to achieve your purpose you need to plan the video very carefully, with at least a structural script even if the talk element is to be spontaneous and chatty. A broad structure might define how the video begins in terms of opening shot, titles, sound effects and so on and specify the different scenes and the order in which they will occur. There has to be a logical coherence, an ordered message and an appropriate sequence that leads the viewer through the information or stages to achieve the end result, whether that is an understanding of health issues in pregnancy or how to set about building a coracle.

The broad sweep of the structure of your coracle instructional video might begin with an opening shot of an old Welsh fisherman working in his coracle and bring his nets and fish to the riverbank with the opening titles superimposed and a suitable piece of music overlaid on the sound track of water and bird sounds. You might have the camera following the fisherman as he unloads his fishing gear, packs it away and then carries his coracle on his back, taking it to its resting place while a voice-over talks about the ancient tradition of coracle building and fishing. The camera might then cut to the presenter who continues the narrative and informs the viewer about what they are to enjoy in the next 40 minutes or so. There might be an interview with the old fisherman, asking him about the traditions of coracle use and building. This might be followed by a drive to the workshop where the tradition of coracle building is still carried on, a chat to the coracle builder, then an extended piece of filming which could show the basic steps and perhaps include either the presenter or some other person being shown how to build their own coracle step-by-step. The film might end with the launching and testing of the coracle (including lessons of how to control it) and information about how to find out more or where you can get supplies, instruction and so on.

Planning

Clearly this is merely the 'vision' around which a more detailed scripting process can take place: planning done on locations, persons to be in the film, camera shots and angles, sound tracks, costs and fees and so on. What is important is that you have a conception at the beginning of the end product as something which is engaging and interesting as well as informational and instructive.

For most video productions, there will be a lengthy process of planning and perhaps an even lengthier process of filming and editing before your product is complete, though I did manage myself to make a 15-minute instructional film as a solo operator (filming and also taking part) to be used within an adult education course of a self-sufficient smallholding. This was made on an ancient reel-to-reel Sony portable video outfit the size of an old-fashioned reel-to-reel tape recorder with a large video camera attached and was, naturally, in black and white.

Although lacking the sophistication of editing facilities I think I made a useful film which did its job. The title was simply a shot of the signboard at the end of the driveway of the old country house where the self-sufficiency couple lived, followed by a sweep of the general view of the place. To take part in the film I set up a shot then walked into the picture and talked about the place and what I had come to see, using the same method to interview the owner, and at the end of the interview suggested we went to view the pigs, at which point we both walked out of shot. I then turned the camera off and set up the next shot at the pigsty – and so on. Of course it was amateurish when compared to television films, but it fulfilled its purpose in being able to bring the experience of that self-sufficient smallholding into the classroom to be informative and a starting off point for the consideration of various issues relevant to the course.

Duplication

Once you have made your film you will need to have copies made and presented in cases with a printed insert. There are companies that will produce these from your master tape in modest quantities. Try your local trade telephone directory for details. See also Useful addresses at the end of this chapter.

Electronic books

The latest, hottest form of publishing is the electronic book with a market potential according to DigiTrends.net of £1.5 billion by 2005. Microsoft® have made their reader software available on free download (http://www.microsoft.com/reader) while Barnes and Noble, one of the large internet booksellers, give away free Glassbook Reader software. Having said that, the electronic book comprises a number of different products, many of them having the personal computer as their common denominator. An electronic book can be in the form of a $3^1/2''$ floppy disk, a CD-ROM, or a file transmitted over the internet. It can take the form of plain text, be configured as chapters between which you can move at the click of a mouse, as web pages, or in some very fancy formats including moving images, flash, video clips and so on. What you will be able to produce will depend very largely on the programs you have access to and your skills in using the more technical aspects of such programs, including web skills.

There are a number of new formats becoming established based on special reading devices, such as the Rocket Book, a hand-held device of book size and just 22 ounces in weight which holds 4,000 pages of text (equivalent to about ten novels). E-books for the Rocket Reader (some 3,600+ titles) are purchased and downloaded into the device from a secure website at a cost of around \$14–\$23 each. A number of other approaches, such as Glassbooks, have taken the path of a software platform for use in PCs and free e-books are available for a number of palm-top computers such as Hewlett Packard's Jordana and Casio's Cassiopeia and no doubt by the time this old-style book gets onto the shelves the picture will have changed considerably.

Creating an electronic book

Since, therefore, this is a very fast moving area it is unrealistic to attempt to give information on state-of-the-art possibilities, but the basic information given here should enable you to make a start in this field.

The simplest way to produce an electronic book is simply to transfer the computer files of your chapters onto a floppy disk. This is best done in Word for Windows® as possibly the most universally available program due to Microsoft's overarching dominance in software; however, it does limit the availability of your product, excluding those who do not have the program on their computer or have a version too old to read the one you have used to create your files. You should be able to get a substantial book of 60,000 or more words onto a standard high-density disk.

Once you have created the master copy of your files on a floppy disk, all you have to do (and this applies to an electronic book on disk created by any other program) is to copy the disk when an order arrives, stick a label on it, pop in a board-backed or bubble-pack envelope and post it off. You can also make your product look more professional by creating a cover for it designed on an A4 sheet divided into six equal squares then folded down the middle long-ways then into thirds to form an open ended envelope when one end is tucked into the other. Make a mock up and work out which squares to put your title and other information on – and which way up. You then print these out as required either on your inkjet printer in colour or on a laser printer, in black on coloured paper.

For a simple text-only electronic book you might consider the Writer's Dream software program. This requires no programming knowledge whatsoever and simply needs you to place your word processed files for each chapter or section of your book into the program, choosing a colour for the background and creating a contents page from which the reader can click from chapter to chapter. The book can be read on screen or printed out if preferred and does not need any other program in order to access and read it. You can download a free shareware copy of the program from: http://www.bestconnections.co.uk

For a more substantial publication or one which contains photographs or other graphics you will need more space than a floppy disk provides. If you are planning to distribute the book physically rather than via the internet, you will need to add a CD writer to your computer to handle the larger size files. With a CD writer you can, of course, simply provide Word for Windows® files but you will now also be able to utilize one of the programs that make possible more exciting formats which are universally accessible, such as PDF files.

PDF files

Adobe Acrobat PDF files are becoming the most commonly used format, with the Acrobat Reader program being available as a free file which can be added to your CD to be downloaded by the reader. This format can also be delivered via the internet either from a secure website or by e-mail using an autoresponder. Other formats and programs you can use include

HTML files for which a suitable program is Hyper Maker. Once you have saved your Word or other files as HTML files Hyper Maker turns them into an .EXE file – an executable file that can be run from the receiving computer. You can also include a password in this system which enables you to allow access to, say, the first chapter then denies access to the rest until the book is paid for and the relevant password obtained. With a secure server on your website and a merchant account this means virtually immediate access for the purchaser and, if you also have an autoresponder installed, the whole process can be automated so that you don't even know about the sale until you see the money in your bank account. Another such program worth looking at is Neobook, which enables anyone to produce e-books integrating text, images, sound, music, animation, colour etc., to produce stunning multimedia productions.

E-books and the internet

If you are sending your e-book ever the internet you will need to make it 'internet ready' by compressing it into a smaller file size so that it downloads quickly. The most common and popular compression program is WinZip and once you have created your .zip file you need to make it into a 'self-extracting' zip file so that the recipient can read it even if they don't have a zip program on their own computer system. See Useful addresses at the end of this chapter.

Remember, however, despite the exciting possibilities of the internet and e-commerce, that the real, non-electronic world still exists, so you can still sell your e-book on CD-ROM using advertising and the postal system to sell and deliver your product. Having created your e-book and saved it to a master CD-ROM you can either copy these one by one as you need them or have them duplicated for you by specialist firms. Check your local trade telephone directory for details or see Useful addresses below.

Useful addresses

Standard Book Numbering Agency, 12 Dyott Street, London, WC1A 1DF.

Axis Multidata, Maestro House, 4 Fir Road, Bramhall, Stockport, Cheshire, SK7 2NP. Tel: 0161 440 9877. Fax: 0161 439 5108.

ABC Graphics Ltd, Centrepoint House, 14 The Green, Haslam, Chesterfield, Derbyshire S41 0LJ. Tel: 01246 221009. Fax: 01246 233144. E-mail: john@centrespot.co.uk

Downsoft Ltd, Downsway House, Epsom Road, Ashtead, Surrey KT21 1LD. Tel: 01372 272422. Fax: 01372 276122. E-mail: work@downsoft. force9.co.uk

Fair View Music, Great Gutter Lane West, Willerby, Hull HU10 6DP. Tel: 01482 653116. Fax: 01482 654667. E-mail: keith@fairview-music. demon.co.uk

Some short-run book printers and book packagers

Antony Rowe Ltd, Bumper's Farm, Chippenham, Wiltshire SN14 6LH. Tel: 01249 659705. Fax: 01249 443103. E-mail: 100616.40@ compuserve.com

Ex-Libris Press Book Production, 1 The Shambles, Bradford on Avon, Wiltshire BA15 1JS. Tel: 01225 863595. E-mail: roger.jones@ex-librisbooks.co.uk

CopyPlus of Monmouth, Hadnock Road, Monmouth, Wales NP25 3NQ. Tel: 01600 772600. Fax: 01600 712896. E-mail: wmp@copyplus. demon.co.uk

Juma Printing & Publishing, 1st Floor, Trafalgar Works, 44 Wellington Street, Sheffield, South Yorkshire S1 4HD. Tel: 0114 272 0915. Fax: 0114 278 6550. E-mail: Mlacey5816@aol.com

Intype London Ltd, Units 3–4 Elm Grove Industrial Estate, Elm Grove, Wimbledon, London SW19 4HE. Tel: 0208 947 7863. Fax: 0208 947 3652. E-mail: intype@btconnect.com

The Book Company, PO Box 243, Ipswich, Suffolk IP4 1DD. Tel: 01473 212104. Fax: 01473 212105.

The Book Factory, 35–37 Queensland Road, London N7 7AH. Tel: 0207 700 1000. Fax: 0207 700 3569.

Specialist printers

Speedprint, Gladiator Works, Gladiator Street, Forest Hill, London SE23 1NA. Tel: 0208 690 8282. Fax: 0208 690 5167.

Mutual Advantage, 397 Old Road, Clacton on Sea, Essex CO15 3RJ. Tel: 01255 473605.

Catford Copy Centre, 3 Bellingham Road, Catford, London SE6 4PY. Tel: 0208 695 0101. Fax: 0208 695 0566.

Paul Clark Printing, Park Lane, Toppesfield, Essex CO9 4DQ. Tel: 01787 237801. Fax: 01787 237733.

Cornerstone Print, 1 Cecil Court, Pegrams Road, Staple Tye, Harlow, Essex CM18 7QR. Tel: 01279 437851.

Centreprint Direct, Unit 1, Lanesfield Drive, Ettingshall, Wolverhampton, West Midlands WV4 6UA. Tel: 01902 402693. Fax: 01902 491794.

Magazine printers

Rowe The Printers, 3c Guildford Industrial Estate, Guildford Road, Hayle, Cornwall TR27 4QZ. Tel: 01736 756435. E-mail: jg@rowe-printers.demon.co.uk

TPL Printing, Unit 111, Hartlebury Trading Estate, Nr Kidderminster, Worcestershire, DY10 4JB. Tel: 01299 251360. E-mail: steve.evans@tplprinter.co.uk

Garnet Dickinson Print, Eastwood Works, Fitzwilliam Road, Rotherham, Yorkshire S65 1JU. Tel: 01709 364721.

The Magazine Printing Company, 25 Mollison Avenue, Brimsdown, Enfield, Middlesex EN3 7NT. Tel: 0208 805 5000. E-mail: magprint@compuserve.com

The Norman W Hardy Group, 112 Bermondsey Street, London SE1 3TX. Tel: 0207 378 1579. Fax: 0207 378 6422. E-mail: info@ normanhardygroup.com

This is a number of independent printers across the country trading as a group, giving a wide and flexible range of printing services including help and advice with design and other aspects of magazine production.

You can also find a suitable printer (for magazines and other types of printing) through the website of the British Printing Industries Federation at: www.selectprinter.com

Video duplication

Denfield (Video Tapes), 3 Little Heath, Chadwell Heath, Romford, Essex RM6 4XX. Tel: 0208 590 4593.

R T Litho, Units B2/B3 Newton Industrial Estate, Eastern Avenue West, Chadwell Heath, Romford, Essex RM6 5SD. Tel: 0800 298 3633. Fax: 0208 599 8963. E-mail: ricky@vhsblank.co.uk

Mediamagic, The Unit, 257/259 Oldfield Lane North, Greenford, Middlesex UB6 8PX. Tel: 0208 578 0461.

CD duplication

CD Express Ltd, Unit 3, Oldfield Industrial Estate, Oldfield Road, Maidenhead, Berkshire SL6 1CA. Tel: 0800 169 1755. Fax: 0800 167 4776. E-mail: sales@cd-express.co.uk

R T Litho, Units B2/B3 Newton Industrial Estate, Eastern Avenue West, Chadwell Heath, Romford, Essex RM6 5SD. Tel: 0800 298 3633. Fax: 0208 599 8963. E-mail: ricky@vhsblank.co.uk

Website addresses

Rocket Books: http://www.rocketbooks.com

Glassbooks: http://glassbook.com

Adobe Acrobat: http://www.adobe.com

Hyper Maker: http://www.bersoft.com

Neobook: http://www.neosoftware.com

WinZip: http://www.winzip.com

Note: Readers in countries other than the UK should consult the appropriate trade and business directories for providers of equivalent information and services.

7 | MARKETING YOUR PRODUCT

What this chapter will be focusing on is marketing in the broadest sense for, while many people equate marketing simply with selling it is, in fact, a key activity – *the* key activity – in any business. Effective marketing is crucial to the success of any business and actual selling is only one small part of the marketing effort. Indeed, I would go as far as saying that without marketing there *is* no business.

What is marketing?

The reason why marketing is so crucial to any enterprise is that it encompasses the whole process of getting your product or service to the end user – the market. This means that it includes the decisions about what you are going to charge, who you are going to sell to, how you are going to reach them, what methods of payment you will accept, what style, image and approach your enterprise is going to promote, how the product or service is to be delivered – and even (perhaps most important) what product or service you are going to produce. Let's look at each of these aspects in turn.

Pricing

What you can charge for your product depends at least to some extent on the general parameters for that type of product in the marketplace. Thus, as we noticed in the previous chapter, most people have a pretty good idea of what they expect to pay for commonly purchased items like books, magazines and newspapers, so that puts a limit on your pricing policy. Moreover, your book or magazine has to be competitively priced and people will notice if your thin, 96-page hardback is priced at £16.95 when it sits on the shelf next to a best-selling blockbuster of 350 pages at a mere

£10.99. When you present your product in a less familiar form and sell it direct to a carefully targeted audience then that price restraint may no longer operate in quite the same way. That is why you can get £5 or £20 for 12 A4 sheets of paper in the form of a newsletter which would be unlikely to make a single sale if it were to be displayed on a newsagent's shelf.

That is the first reason why marketing has to be at the start and heart of your business plans, because what you produce, who you sell it to and how much you charge are crucial factors in your overall profitability. Do you want to sell 1,000 copies of a newsletter for £120 a year or 2,857 magazines each month at £3.50 each? That is a marketing decision and in making it you have to consider all sorts of other things such as the cost of getting these sales in terms of mailshots or advertising for the first, or discounts to retailers and wholesalers and the cost of distribution for the second.

Who to sell to

One of the big mistakes many small publishers make is to go for a product that appeals to everybody on the grounds that this will make for higher sales volume and ease of marketing. It doesn't work like that. The product that suits everybody is bought by nobody. Well, not quite, but in order to sell a product that suits everyone you have to be producing something fairly bland and you have to get it to the attention of the whole of the marketplace – an exceedingly expensive operation. One mainstream magazine publisher is on record as saying that he would not contemplate a new magazine launch on a budget of less than £1 million. On the other hand, a product aimed at a small and easily identifiable sector of the population, such as dentists, teachers or motor cycle owners for example, will have a more targeted, in-depth content and be more desirable to the market segment it is aimed at – and they can be reached much more easily and economically through specialist publications and similar avenues (like trade or professional associations).

It is important to think about who you want to sell to *before you decide what it is you want to sell*. It will be a far harder marketing exercise to sell a book on saving money to the poor than to sell a book to the rich about making even more money. In other words, what you need to look for is a market which has discretionary money to spend on the kind of thing you want to sell – that is, they have surplus money after paying for essentials that they will enjoy spending on non-necessities like your publishing products, while those less well-off, having little or no discretionary income, are struggling too hard to pay their bills to be able to afford to buy your excellent and even desirable book which would help them to save money. That may be tough, but it is life and the reality is that you must target people with money rather than those who can't afford to buy from you.

Getting paid

If you are following the conventional publishing route of selling through the book or periodical trade, you will be collecting your money by sending out invoices and statements and, as a small publisher, you will find that it takes a long time to collect what is owed to you. There is also likely to be an inverse relationship between the size of your customer and the speed with which they will settle your bill. Add to that the huge discounts that some powerful chains can demand and the time, effort and postage you will spend trying to collect small amounts for single copy orders, and you will begin to realize how difficult it is to pursue publishing by the traditional route when you are a small publisher.

A tip here: if you are not predominantly publishing for the trade you will nonetheless find yourself picking up the odd order for single copies of your publications via Whitaker's Information Service or customer requests to their local bookshop – do not invoice these, but send a pro-forma invoice payable before you send out the book. This will not make you popular, but it will save you untold hassle and trouble following up the small amounts you will end up being owed. Do this only if you are not dependent on the trade for the bulk (or even a substantial part) of your business. I would also advise, from my own experience, adding to your conditions of trade that no returns are accepted other than when there has been a genuine mistake or the book is faulty – and print this on your invoices.

The ideal situation for a small publisher is one in which the customer pays up-front for your book or magazine/newsletter subscription, giving you a healthy cash flow of cheques, postal orders and credit card transactions. 'Cash with order' is the key to a healthy, trouble-free business in small-scale publishing and, since you are likely to be marketing through newspaper and magazine advertisements, direct mail and through sending information directly to your own customer lists, this should present no problem.

Style and image

The style, image and approach of your company are important contributory factors in your success. Do you want to be 'cheap and cheerful', aiming for high volumes of low-priced items, or do you aim to present an image of solidity and smooth professional competence that will give reassurance to those who, you hope, are about to part with large cheques in return for your offerings? What kind of 'voice' will be appropriate to talk to your perceived market segment? Detached and urbane? Friendly and chatty? Eager and enthusiastic? Hard-hitting and full of lavish promises? These considerations should lead you to identify your USP (Unique Selling Proposition) as a publisher – the thing that distinguishes you from all your competitors which will lead people to do business with you more than with them. Your USP may be based on best value (perhaps you always offer a free book with every two ordered), your two-year guarantee, the fact that your books are the only ones recommended or approved by some prestigious body, that your products are environmentally friendly, or a proportion of your profits is donated to a worthy cause of which your readers would approve. Spend some time thinking about what distinguishes you and makes your company or your range of products unique and place that at the centre of all your marketing. Make sure that your USP is firmly focused on customer benefits so that potential buyers will see a clear personal advantage in buying from you.

Reaching your customers

How will you contact your customers? Will they buy through intermediaries such as retail shops? Will there be an intermediate layer of wholesalers and distributors? Will you send out information to specialized mailing lists? Take advertisements in magazines or newspapers? Aim to be a dot.com company, selling and perhaps delivering over the internet? Just as you have to decide how to get your sales message across to your chosen target market, so you have to decide, as part of your marketing and business plan, how the products are to be delivered. The options here are basically:

- using the retail/wholesale book distribution chain
- selling through non-traditional retail outlets such as garages, garden centres, pet shops, DIY stores and other non-book retailers

- delivering by post or carrier
- sending electronic publications via e-mail or from a secure website.

Having considered all these dimensions of marketing you should begin to have a clear idea of how your business is likely to work in practice. Most businesses that fail are those which have not considered marketing seriously or worked out realistically how their products will reach their intended audience. Very many of the most successful businesses, on the other hand, are those which have decided on an attractive market with the requisite discretionary income and one that they can reach economically and with comparative ease. Having identified the market, they then consider what that market wants (note: 'wants' rather than 'needs' – people are more likely to buy from desire, not from a sense of necessity) and begin to plan how they can produce products that fulfil their customers' desires and aspirations.

As an example of a marketing plan, consider my own approach to the teaching profession as a specialized market.

Having run a very successful specialized service called 'The Escape Committee' to help teachers change career, I then sold the career-change magazine *Escape*, which had evolved from my initial newsletter-based service. The company that bought the magazine eventually failed and I recently decided to return to that market again, believing it still to have considerable potential.

My marketing plan this time was to bring together all that I knew about career change for teachers into what I describe as *The Escape Kit*, trading on the initial concept which was still remembered by many teachers. This was put together as a 140pp A4 manual and was also available on disk as an electronic book. The market would be reached (as before) by a classified advert in the *Times Educational Supplement*, enquirers being sent a leaflet with details of the kit and copies of a number of press articles mentioning our new endeavour plus a FREEPOST envelope for orders.

Since, even at £29.95 including postage and packaging (P&P) (and £19.00 including P&P for the electronic book version), this would not be very profitable, it was essential that I found a number of other publications that could be offered to purchasers (and non-purchasing enquirers) as back-end sales. At the time of writing these back-end products are limited to a course on earning from feature and article writing, an import/export course, a course on the commercial possibilities of the internet, a manual on marketing, a business opportunities newsletter, a course on setting up your own stage school, a course on making an income from property, and a course on travel writing. All of those, except the writing course, have been written or produced by others with whom we have negotiated either royalty payments or an agency agreement. We have in the pipeline plans for a directory of unusual or alternative careers for teachers, a course on setting up a tutoring agency and other courses and guides to self-employed possibilities.

These will all be sold by regularly mailing the growing list of enquirers and buyers for *The Escape Kit* as we have found that repeated mailings bring in additional sales, with an eventual conversion ratio of around 34 per cent of sales to enquiries. Once we have built up the line of suitable products and a regular mailing schedule, this niche market will be a solid and significant contribution to our profits. We are following a similar pattern for another of our developing niche markets based on the growing list of writers who have bought our writing course. Our back-end products for this market will be a range of other specialist writing courses, such as copywriting, travel writing, self-publishing and so on.

Assessing the demand

Practically everything in this chapter is connected to, if not an intrinsic part of, marketing and making an assessment of the demand for your intended product is part of the process of deciding what to publish – hopefully before you rush ahead and produce an item no one is likely to want. How can you assess the demand for a product that isn't even written or produced?

The first step is to see if there are other similar products in the marketplace already. If there are, be encouraged rather than dismayed, because the fact that those products have established themselves shows that there is a market, and if there is a market, then you can win a share of it provided your product offers something unique or is at least a good value product which can compete against those already available.

Send for information about these products or look at them if they are available in the shops. Try to analyse them for content, value, uniqueness and appeal so that you can plan your product in such a way that it will be better, offer more and be uniquely different or meet the buyer's needs more effectively.

Conduct some kind of survey either by sending a simple questionnaire to existing customers asking if they would be interested in the product you are contemplating or canvass the opinions of leading people in the field. Try writing a letter to an appropriate newspaper or professional journal asking for feedback about the proposal (that is how we launched our *Escape* newsletter for teachers over 15 years ago). Take this a stage further and offer readers a free report on the subject (perhaps in return for a couple of postage stamps). The response should give some idea of the scale of interest, indicating whether it would be worthwhile to go ahead with the full publication and providing a databank of people already interested who might buy the publication when it is produced.

A free report is the first component in 'funnel marketing' – one US mail order guru calls this 'concatenation' – which means the same thing but suffers from the obscurity of the word, while the term funnel marketing is descriptive of the process that good direct marketers use. You start at the narrow end of the funnel by offering a free or very low cost product in order to draw in the largest number of interested prospects who are then offered a larger publication (perhaps a book or manual) which expands on the subject of interest. Once in the funnel they are then offered a more substantial publication such as a part-work or study course, or the opportunity to subscribe to a specialist newsletter or magazine, bringing on-going profits.

This is a refinement on the notion of a back-end product – the product which you offer to buyers as a follow-on sale. You can see that offering a carefully planned sequence of related publications rising in price and value is a much more powerful marketing approach than simply offering a haphazard selection of other publications that you just happen to have available. It should also now become apparent that a planned marketing strategy must lie at the heart of any small publishing enterprise that wants to be successful. Developing a customer base in a niche market makes it much easier to know what products you should be publishing and gives you an easy and effective way to assess what demand there will be for new products.

Distribution

Just as marketing is the key component of any publisher's business plan, so the choice of distribution for the products is significant – in fact, it will determine the nature of the business. That being so, it makes sense to consider this before going on to look at the more detailed aspects of advertising, public relations, copywriting and so on.

Distribution can be broadly divided into two major choices. The first is to follow the normal trade route and distribute through the book trade or other retail outlets, while the alternative is to sell your products direct to the customer or end user and thus maintain total control over marketing and selling. There is another option which can be added to the direct marketing approach, that of using agents to sell, usually in addition to your own sales, but sometimes as a sole means of distribution. It is highly likely as a small, specialist publisher, that you will choose some variant of the direct sales approach, but first we will examine the trade route to see what it offers and what problems it presents to the new small publisher.

The trade route

Books

Although there are some differences in the trade distribution of magazines and books, both share the same basic logistical problem: how do you get 3,000 copies of your book spread throughout the country and displayed on the book shop shelves and how do you get 50,000 of your little magazine onto newsagents' shelves throughout the country so that people can see them, pick them up, browse and buy?

Clearly, you cannot effectively do that by yourself. That is why there are specialist distribution companies for newspapers and magazines and wholesalers for books.

In the case of books your distributor's representatives (assuming you can find a distributor – most will not find it worth their while to handle your account) will take the jackets or covers of your book around the trade book shops along with the dozens of other new offerings from the many other publishers he or she represents. For a brief half minute your book is flashed before the eyes of the buyer who may decide to order maybe three copies – six if it is a big shop and you are lucky. So far so good, but you are not home and dry at that stage. Why? However it may have seemed to you, you do not have a firm sale. In the book trade the convention is that books are bought essentially on sale or return. In other words, having decided to take into stock six copies of your book, the bookseller may send them back for credit if they remain unsold in nine months' time. What is more, the bookseller may take some months to pay your invoice, and that often after several reminders. You, of course, finding yourself with unsold stock of some 450 books cannot go back to your printer and ask for a refund because you have not sold the books! No other trade or business operates on the antiquated system that underpins the book trade.

Magazines

So perhaps it would be better to think of publishing a magazine to avoid such problems? No such luck. The problems faced by small magazine publishers are equally horrendous. First, you have to find a distributor to handle your magazine, which is extremely difficult, so much so that an association of small magazine publishers in the 1980s spent a great deal of energy and time trying without success to find a small distributor who would handle their joint titles. But, even assuming you can find a distributor, what happens? Your magazines are thinly distributed at random into the various deliveries that go out to newsagents. Magazines that are still on the rack on their sell-by date are bundled up and returned to the distributor for pulping, so of the copies that reached the shops, some 60 per cent are likely to be returned unsold. 'Why not,' I asked the group, 'send 25,800 out in the first place to match what appears to be the demand?' Sadly, they related, it doesn't seem to work like that. When they send out fewer copies the proportion of returns seems to stay roughly the same, leading to spiralling decreases in circulation. Only the advertising revenue makes such magazines pay – and if circulation is diminishing, then advertising will dry up too. As for selling to the big newsagency and bookstore chains, you will have all that plus being screwed down to a price that barely makes your operation viable.

You will gather from the above that I am not enthused of the book trade route for the marketing of small publishers' products! Some tackle it with some modest degree of success, but for most it is a nightmare. I recommend you consider more direct avenues and keep the whole process under your own control.

Advertising and promotion

If you have followed the guidance already given about looking to a niche market and providing what seems to be wanted by that market, then your advertising and promotion plan will be fairly obvious. For example, your guide to motor cycle racetracks in the UK will find buyers through classified adverts in the three dozen or so motor cycling magazines listed in *Willings Press Guide* (or the equivalent in countries other than the UK). From the same source you will easily find the obvious magazines to place classified adverts for subscribers to your newsletter about maximizing profits in hairdressing and beauty salons. There are plenty of magazines through which you can easily reach teachers for educational products and golfers are easily contactable through a score or more golf publications.

Beware of advertising space sales people! They will attempt to persuade you to do one of two things, if not both: first, to buy as large a display advert as they can sell you and, second, to book a series to obtain a discount. Now, while it is true that you can benefit from having a discount, it is not true, as they often assert, that you have to run an advert several times before it begins to work. *If your first insertion gets no response, then the second and third won't either*. Take one insertion, then kill it if there is no (or too little) response. The golden rule is always to test the efficacy of a new advertising medium by running a classified advert for one insertion. If it works well, run it on a continuous basis until the results begin to fall off, then either switch to another publication for a while or try new wording and a fresh approach.

Only try display advertising once you have tested the viability of that publication by using classified adverts successfully. If you are astute, you can do better than the advertising sales person's discount offer. Here is the secret: make up display advertisements in several sizes then send them with a covering letter to the advertising manager telling him or her that when they find themselves with 'remnant' space (advertising space left unsold just as they are about to go to press), to put it in at 80 per cent discount. That's right! You offer to pay £60 for a £300 advertising space – *and you will very often get it*. You could be even cheekier and send an undated cheque for the amount you want to pay and tell them to put it in whenever they have a suitable unsold space. Believe me, a cheque in the hand is worth more than a difficult prospect on the end of a telephone line – they will be sorely tempted to date the cheque and take your offer! If you can pull off that trick half a dozen times a year with different magazines you will save yourself a thousand or two in advertising costs.

Set up a simple system of recording the results of your adverts. Always key each advert by including a code in the address that will tell you where and when the advert appeared from which you are getting each sale. Your code might appear after your trading name something like (TES/3N2000) which would indicate that the advert which generated the sale was in the *Times Educational Supplement* on 3 November 2000. This is easier to check than a straightforward number or letter coding, but choose the system or style that suits you – and record and analyse the results so that you can tell which adverts are profitable and which are not.

It was Lord Lever, the soap magnate, who complained that 50 per cent of his advertising didn't work, but if he knew which 50 per cent it was, he would have become rich much more quickly! That points up another important aspect of advertising: don't be bamboozled by advertising people into 'creative' or 'clever' advertising that is fun to read and look at but which does not produce measurable results. David Ogilvy, the great guru of modern advertising, said:

'For all their research, most advertisers never know for sure whether their advertisements sell. Too many other factors cloud the equation. But direct response advertisers, who solicit orders by mail or telephone, know to a dollar how much each advertisement sells. So watch the kind of advertising they do.' (*Ogilvy on Advertising*, Prion Books)

One final word on display advertising: although there is a general direct mail rule that 'the more you tell, the more you sell' (in other words, long copy outsells short copy) the size of a display advertisement does not determine its effectiveness. A full-page advertisement will not produce twice the sales of a half-page advert.

Guerrilla marketing

Press releases

When you are small and operating on a limited budget, you need to learn how to become a guerrilla marketer, finding ways to get publicity and the sales that result from it, for nothing or next-to-nothing. How do you do this? First, by learning to recognize any newsworthy aspects of your publishing activity and of individual publications and maximizing their value by issuing press releases to local and national publications and the radio and TV stations. If written in a suitable style, your press release may be printed in its entirety and unchanged as an article. This will have much more impact than a paid advertisement because editorial matter is seen as more reliable and trustworthy because it is, apparently, independent. Newsworthy items may be the launch of a new book on a 'hot' subject, some unusual aspect of the author, the launching of a new publishing enterprise, the answer to a problem that readers may encounter (answered by your publication) – almost any aspect of your activities and publications can be angled to appear newsworthy. Make sure that your press release carries a resource box at the end giving details of how readers can follow up on the information given, that is by contacting you. One press release, picked up and used by only one of the dozens of publications you have sent it to, will cost less than a small classified advertisement and will be many times more effective.

When you write a press release make sure that you have a strong and newsworthy headline. Get straight to the point and give the whole story in the first few sentences, then if the editor decides it needs to be cut, he or she can lop off the later paragraphs and still have a comprehensible story. You can enhance your press release by including two extra sheets – one with interesting biographical details of the writer to give human interest, and the other in the form of a set of questions that are appropriate to ask about the subject of the press release and, of course, the appropriate answers. From this any journalist can make up a piece which appears to include a live interview.

Free offers

What other kinds of guerrilla marketing can you use? Try making free offers to the readers of the magazines and other publications that target your market. Offer a free report related to the topic of your new publication; offer a second, free book to the first ten or 20 purchasers; produce a free newsletter – preferably an internet-based one as this will cost virtually nothing to deliver by e-mail and will bring details of your publications to the readers along with some interesting information which they will value; offer a special discount to a magazine's readers. Editors love to be able to make offers to their readers and your costs for making them will be minimal.

Letter writing

Write letters to the correspondence columns of target publications. One woman selling health supplements simply wrote a letter telling how she lost weight with a herbal slimming product and she was inundated with hundreds of requests for information and built a thriving business that had cost her nothing but a postage stamp in marketing costs.

Shared mailings

Team up with other people who want to reach the same audience as you do, but with non-competing products, and do a shared mailing to an appropriate mailing list. If you do all the organizing, you could end up getting your information out completely free, making a charge to the others for the service which covers your printing and other costs. You could also arrange to exchange your mailing lists with others to cut costs.

Other ideas

Post information in internet newsrooms, build an opt-in e-mail list and post details of your publications on a website.

Send review copies of your publication to target magazines. Write to the producers of chat shows and other TV and radio programmes suggesting that the topic of your latest publication would make a good item for their show.

Write articles on your chosen topic and offer them to editors, including a resource box – if you are lucky, you get paid, effectively, for them to run your advertising!

Try to have your publication listed or recommended by professional or other appropriate bodies – offer a discount to their members.

Publicity and public relations

Much of what is suggested above falls within the field of publicity and public relations, which are about getting your name and your activities and publications into the public eye. They say that 'all publicity is good publicity' but, clearly, some publicity can be damaging. It takes only one person to make a public complaint about your service or publication to begin to make people think the worst and become wary of dealing with you. Bad publicity must always be counteracted by a very public rebuttal of the complaint with a magnanimous offer to put right what the complainant is unhappy about or to return his or her money or even refund him or her twice what they paid as a goodwill gesture. Your good name is one of your most valuable assets and should be protected at all costs.

As a small publisher I get a fairly large number of press releases and PR mailings from companies large and small and my major conclusion is that the PR industry in this country has yet to learn the first rule of public relations. The rule is that to blow your own trumpet is counter-productive, but to please and excite the recipient by offering some benefit is the only effective kind of public relations. No one, editor or reader, is at all interested in the fact that the XYZ Corporation has appointed Joanna Twizzlestick as their new marketing manager, nor in the details of her meteoric career rise. What they *are* interested in is the fact that she has immediately introduced price cuts across the range of the company's products which will benefit consumers and that each product will now carry a lifetime guarantee. In other words, what PR should be about is trumpeting the benefits for the customer, not in self-regarding puffery that is of no interest or benefit to anyone other than the company and its staff.

Writing advertising copy and sales letters

This is a vast subject that can only be touched on here, but there are some important rules which may help you in taking your first steps in this fascinating area.

1 Don't put your company name and details at the top (read the preceding paragraph again). Put them at the end.

2 Use a serif typeface (the kind with little 'feet') – sans serif (without 'feet') text reduces comprehension by 67 per cent. Don't use lots of different typefaces – keep it simple.

3 Use black text on white or lightly tinted paper.

4 Break up your text into reasonably short paragraphs – large blocks of text discourage reading.

5 Start with a strong headline that attracts attention, preferably spelling out your product's biggest benefit ('Double your money every year with this unique investment strategy') or homing in on a major problem or worry ('Have you ever wondered why so many of your contemporaries are earning more than you?').

6 Focus on the benefits your book or publication will bring into the lives of the readers.

7 Use a direct, personal style. Try visualizing the typical buyer you are aiming at, preferably a person you know, and addressing yourself to them.

8 Use the AIDA formula – Attention, Interest, Desire and Action.

9 Remember that long copy outpulls short copy.

10 Make it clear what you want the reader to do when he or she has read your letter or advert.

11 Include a form or coupon to make response easier and use a FREEPOST address to save them having to find a stamp.

12 Always use a PS. Research shows that people always read the PS in a letter – usually after reading the headline.

13 Always include a time-limited offer – a discount or a free gift, for example – to make the reader take action rather than put it aside until later. In the world of mail order sales, later never comes.

14 Always offer a guarantee ('complete satisfaction or your money back without question').

Mailshots

This is not the place to provide a course in the complex subject of direct mail, however, some useful pointers are:

1 Don't expect sales from a mailshot to be more than 1–2 per cent from a list other than your own customer list. A good customer list, on the other hand, can produce results of 5–12 per cent – I have even had a result of more than 35 per cent from a mailshot to buyers of a unique book offering them a second book on the subject. Drayton Bird, master direct marketer and author of *Commonsense Direct Marketing*, once achieved a return of 51 per cent! Alas, this kind of return is the exception rather than the norm.

2 If renting lists, make sure that you buy from a reputable source and that you know exactly what you are buying, i.e., the list should be recent buyers of similar items to those you are offering.

3 Test a small quantity of any list you are thinking of mailing.

4 Make building up your own mailing list your top priority – this list will be your 'crock of gold', the most valuable property your business will have apart from the publications you produce.

5 Mail your list on a regular basis, mailing your good buyers (the 20 per cent who account for 80 per cent of your sales) around every four to six weeks, the less frequent purchasers every three months or so and the rest once a year, eliminating non-buyers after a number of mailings, but remember that experience suggests many people will only buy from you after several mailings. The American information publisher and direct mail guru Jeffrey Lant recommends mailing people seven times before giving up on them.

You can get a free guide (around 50 pages) to direct mailing lists from HiLite (see Chapter 11) either in book format or as a downloadable e-book. Write or e-mail them for details. Hamilton House publishes a free direct mail newsletter. Contact them and ask to be put on the mailing list. Refer to Chapter 11 for details of mailing list brokers.

Data Protection Agency

If you hold data on individuals for marketing or other purposes – even if not on computer – you will have to register with The Office of the Data Protection Commissioner. Countries other than the UK will have their own equivalent legislation. (See end of chapter for details.)

Your most valuable marketing resource

The most valuable marketing resource that any business has is its list of existing or past customers. It is as good as money in the bank, for it has been established that gaining a new customer costs eight to ten times the cost of approaching an existing customer. Not only so, but provided that your existing customer has had a good buying experience and is pleased with the product he or she has bought from you then buying from you again is more likely than buying from someone else with whom there has been no prior contact or business. In other words, repeat business comes from satisfaction and trust and your best customers will buy from you again and again, with negligible marketing costs and, therefore, a high level of profitability.

Remember, too, the Pareto Principle: that 20 per cent of your customer base will provide 80 per cent of your sales. Sophisticated data processing companies will be able to pinpoint to the penny what each customer has bought and how often. You need not be so exact, but make sure that your system can identify your regular customers so that you can use this principle to best effect. What you should be doing is mailing your best 20 per cent of customers on a frequent basis (perhaps every four to six weeks), your next best 20 to 30 per cent less regularly (say every two to three months) and the rest once a year until you have determined that they have not bought after two or three such mailings.

This means that your customer list is being used effectively, is constantly cleaned by having 'gone aways' taken out and is concentrated by bringing more and more good buying prospects up into the higher reaches of the list as more frequent buyers. A list that is nurtured and used in this way is worth its weight in gold.

Useful addresses

The Office of the Data Protection Commissioner, Wycliffe House, Water Lane, Wilmslow, Cheshire SK9 5AF. Tel: 01625 545700. Fax: 01625 524510. E-mail: mail@dataprotection.gov.uk

Mailing list brokers

Hamilton House Mailings Ltd, Earlstrees Court, Earlstrees Road, Corby, Northamptonshire NN17 4AX. Tel: 01536 399000. Fax: 01536 399012. E-mail: HHMailing@aol.com

HiLite, Ash House, Ash Road, New Ash Green, Longfield, Kent DA3 8SA. Tel: 01474 874848. Fax: 01474 879292. E-mail: info@hilitedms.co.uk. Website: www.hilitedms.co.uk

Profords Associates, Profords House, 56 Earl Howe Road, Holmer Green, High Wycombe, Buckinghamshire HP15 6QT. Tel: 01494 766123.

BOM Ltd, The Mailing List Shop, 14 Fulham High Street, London SW6 3LQ. Tel: 0207 1371 9131. Fax: 0207 371 9151.

Marketscan Ltd, 8 Duke's Court, Chichester, West Sussex PO19 2FX. Tel: 01243 786711. Fax: 01243 779671. E-mail: mktscan@pavilion.co.uk

BRG Direct Ltd, 55 Morrab Road, Penzance, Cornwall TR18 4EX
Tel: 01736 351681. Fax: 01736 350248.

For more brokers contact:

The British List Brokers Association, Springfield House, Princess Street,
Bedminster, Bristol BS3 4EF. Tel: 01272 666900.

Note: Readers in countries other than the UK should consult the
appropriate trade and business directories for providers of equivalent
information and services.

8 | MONEY MATTERS

Since the object of business is to make profits, I make no apologies for the focus of this chapter, nor for the fact that it repeats some of the points that have been touched on already, for they cannot be emphasized too strongly if your publishing business is to be successful. You must maximize your profits.

Selling to those with money

In Chapter 7 the point was made that some people cannot afford to buy the books that would help them to make money so, unless you aim to be a charitable foundation rather than a business, aim to target the comparatively well-off as your potential customers. They are the people who have the discretionary income that will allow them to buy without hesitation something that is of interest to them and that they see to have some value in their lives.

If the benefits of your product are clear enough, big enough and appealing enough then they will write the cheque, pull out their credit card or sign the authorization to let their bank pay out an annual subscription to you every year. You do *not* want customers who drool over your marketing, long to enjoy the benefits of your product but send you cheques that bounce, numbers for credit cards that have reached their limit or who send for the stuff, read or copy it quickly and send it back for a refund. You want people who buy without hesitation, are pleased to have your publication on their shelf and who will respond to your subsequent offers, buying from you again and again. Only those with comfortable discretionary income will fulfil that requirement.

How can you be sure that your prospects will match that profile? Quite simply, by renting mailing lists that identify high earning individuals who are used to buying by mail and who have bought something similar to the product you have to sell, and by placing your advertising in the kind of magazines that comfortably-off and rich people read. It's that simple.

Choosing a product and format

Your choice of product should be determined by a number of factors, not simply by some vague desire to produce what appeals to you. What you produce must meet the desires of a specific and identifiable group of people with the discretionary income to buy the product. In other words, identify a group of financially affluent people you can easily reach by advertising or direct mail and *create a product that specifically meets their needs* (or, more exactly, their *desires*).

Having identified the product in a general sense, you must then decide what format will be most appealing to the buyers and most profitable to you as publisher. The formula you are looking for here is *low cost, high perceived value*. Since, as publishers, we are in the information business, that is fairly easy to fulfil, for the production costs of information are low, while the perceived value can be extremely high – as much as several hundred times the production cost.

Format and price are closely related. As pointed out earlier, perception of value has something (but not everything) to do with the format chosen. If you want to maximize your income in publishing you will not be likely to choose either a newspaper or magazine format nor a paperback or hardback book, but will look at the possibilities offered by newsletters, special reports and information in electronic media such as computer disks, CD-ROMS and downloadable files accessed via a secure website.

What is also important is that the information product you supply should not be something readily available in large book stores or the local newsagent. Your product must be uniquely created to meet the unmet needs and desires of your target prospects. You must deal in highly specialist niche markets in order to be successful. If there were several paperback books easily available in book shops telling teachers how to escape from teaching into another career, there would be little room in the marketplace for my *Escape Kit* guide sold by mail order at just short of £30. If there were a decent magazine on the news-stands telling people how to set up and run a small home business and supply a continuous stream of good ideas for this, my *Great Ideas* newsletter would not readily sell at a subscription cost of £47.

There are a large number of books on careers and getting a new job, but there is nothing that exactly matches the specific needs of my customers, nor would any of the other publications offer a listening ear and free advice to purchasers as I am able to do because I am operating on a small, personal scale. Likewise there are several news-stand magazines on small business but, since most are advertising-led by the necessity of surviving in a cut-throat market, most focus on franchising, as only the franchised business opportunities have the financial clout to spend large sums advertising in the magazines. My *Great Ideas* newsletter gives people ideas on how to start their own small enterprises on a shoestring, tells them which schemes are worthwhile, which are scams to avoid and can afford to be independent because it is not reliant on advertising but on those £47 subscriptions which guarantee that our loyalty is to the subscribers and not with advertisers with big chequebooks.

A newsletter, which can cost as little as £7 to £10 to produce and distribute, can be sold at a subscription many times that cost. American direct mail guru Bill Myers advises: 'As a minimum, to be profitable a mail order product needs to sell for at least eight times its cost. Many successful products sell for 30 times cost or more.' (*301 Direct Mail Tips, Techniques & Secrets: An Inside Guide To Direct Mail Marketing*). Computer disk-based publications, together with CD-ROMS are examples of this high ratio between cost and sales price, for computer disks cost around 23p when bought in bulk, with CD-ROMs costing between 50p and £1.50, depending on the quantities involved and whether they are copied as required on your own computer with a CD ROM writer or commercially produced from your master disk. E-books, software and other compilations on $3^1/_2''$ disk will easily sell to specialist audiences for anything between £5 and £20, giving a mark-up of nearly 8,000 per cent at the top of that price range. Similarly a CD-ROM can sell for anything between £10 and £50 (and sometimes much more, depending on the perceived value of the specialist information it contains), showing a mark-up of 1,000 per cent or more. Best of all, an e-book delivered by e-mail or from a secure website has absolutely zero production cost, so selling just one is profitable and the whole sales price is profit.

Consider, too, how the value of the printed word is seen when wrapped in 'special report' status or presented as a study course in a ring binder. Not only are these formats seen as justified in having a higher price (a ring-bound study course or specialist report could sell for anything between

£20 and £120 – sometimes more – while costing only £2.50 to £5 to produce) than conventional books, but they lend themselves to low capital means of production as they can be laser printed and bound on demand as one-off productions or copied on commercial quality photocopiers and bound by your printers in small batches of 20 to 25. This method cuts out the need for the relatively large print runs that conventional books need to achieve realistic pricing and frees up or reduces the need for capital, which means that you can produce a range of publications for the same or less cost than publishing and printing one hardback or paperback book. Publishing on demand is undoubtedly part of the answer to the problems facing small specialist publishers, enabling them to survive and flourish in niche markets that are not going to be attractive to the major publishing houses.

How your publication can become a goldmine

While it is generally the case that your first sale to a customer is likely to lead to a loss (which is acceptable as the cost of gaining a new customer) and that a single product business will soon go out of business, what has been outlined in the above section provides a strategy that can enable you to defy those normal conditions of publishing.

If the product you decide on is substantial enough and relatively highly priced (yet still providing high perceived value) it is possible to survive and flourish as a one-publication business. The secret lies in specializing in a particular niche market that can be reached easily with a product seen as indispensable or unique and which provides a sufficiently high margin to make the project profitable.

Consider the economics. Suppose that your niche publication is sold in ring-binder format at £49. If you sell by attracting enquirers by placing classified advertisements in appropriate journals, your monthly sales figures and promotional costs might be:

Sales of 20 publications @ £49		£980
8 classified adverts at an average price of £40	£240	
100 information packages @ 80p sent out to enquirers	£80	
20 publications sent out @ £9 (£5 production + £4 P&P)	£180	
	£500	£500
Gross Profit		£480

The assumptions here are that the journals you will be advertising in will be monthly ones – clearly the overall income would increase if some, at least, were weekly – and that you will convert 20 per cent of enquiries into sales, which is a not unreasonable expectation, and by following up those who do not buy you might be able to achieve a higher sales-to-enquiry ratio (one of my own products, as mentioned in the previous chapter, achieves a ratio of 34 per cent sales-to-enquiries by doing so). These figures would suggest certainly that this project is profitable in its own right, though, unless you can find a considerable number of other ways to advertise or add a regular direct mail campaign to your advertising, it would hardly give you a living. Nevertheless, if your publication could justify a higher price, say £75, it would make a considerable difference to the end results, providing that price resistance does not set in at the higher price. A £75 price would raise your profits to £1,000. Getting the optimum price clearly has a very significant impact on the overall profitability of a project.

If you get your marketing strategy right, whether with classified adverts or direct mail campaigns, you should find, as a rule of thumb, that £1 spent should return £2. If results are markedly poorer than that then you need to test various aspects of your campaign to see what needs to be adjusted.

Should you choose a newsletter project, the prospects are even brighter, for even allowing for subscribers who drop out after their first year's subscription, the renewals should provide you with a growing residual income.

Applying the same set of figures as above, i.e. your newsletter sells at the same price, your advertising costs are the same and your fulfilment costs similar, your newsletter would make you a gross profit of £480 for every

20 subscriptions. After 12 months of such promotion you would have a subscriber base of 240 and would be making £5,760 a year.

A tip here is to ensure that you set up your subscriptions on the basis of bank standing orders which has the dual advantage that, like using a credit card, people feel that they are not actually spending money (or at least they don't feel the pain of it at the time) and, because of both the desire to continue enjoying your publication and the apathy factor which makes them forget to cancel, they will tend to continue automatically into at least the second year.

In your second year then, with the same level of promotion, your end of year profits will be £10,560. This will comprise the same £5,760 from 12 months of new promotion + £4,800 from existing subscribers (assuming a 50 per cent renewal rate and deducting only the fulfilment cost of £9 per subscription). In the third year you could count on further increase in profits from a new 240 subscribers plus 120 of last year's new subscribers and 60 who remain from the first year. Depending, of course, on how vital your subscribers consider your newsletter to be, you may fare better than this and, of course, you can step up the level of your advertising and promotion to build your subscription list faster.

Add to this the fact that specialist newsletters can command much higher prices than the example used here (remember you should be creating a project designed for those who can easily afford the subscription level you choose). At £75 the above figures become very much more attractive – you would be making a nice little income of over £20,000 a year from a subscriber base of just over 400 subscribers. Rework the figures and see!

Add to these figures a little selective advertising from those eager to reach your specialist readership – say the equivalent of four pages an issue at a modest £50 a page – and you can add a further £2,400 of almost pure extra profit over 12 monthly issues. And, of course, you will be selling other items to your readers through your pages – books, reports, services or whatever, and quietly adding an extra couple of thousand to your profits.

Now, a newsletter earning a mere £28,200 may be laughable by the standards of the big newsletter publishers, but what we are looking at here is essentially a part-time project run from home with nothing other than a brain, some basic writing and editing skills, and a home PC! What is more, the potential profits are far greater once your circulation climbs to even a modest 1,000 subscribers, providing an increase in income far in excess of any additional work involved.

Maximizing your profits

Maximizing your profits is not simply achieved by selling more product, for profitability is best gained by combining a number of congruent strategies. As has been pointed out by better marketers than myself, if you can increase your turnover by 10 per cent, your profits (providing that your overheads do not increase) will be a multiple of that 10 per cent, so you may increase your income by a third just by getting 10 per cent more business. The effects on your profits are stupendous – as you will see shortly.

There are three basic ways to increase your business. First, by getting more new customers, second by selling to your existing customers more often, and third, by selling more expensive products to your existing customers. Now, it is a well-established fact that getting new customers is the most expensive way of increasing business and, while you must always be seeking to build up your customer base, this is not likely to be immediately profitable – indeed, it is likely to cost you. However, imagine the effect on your business if just two and a half per cent of your existing customers bought another product from you, and another two and a half per cent were persuaded to buy a more expensive (and therefore more profitable) package from you. This would be the equivalent of increasing your business volume by seven and a half per cent, but the increase in your *profits* is likely to be more than 75 per cent! Here is how it works:

Assume that you initially got 800 customers from a mailing of 40,000 ul a cost of £12,000 (£300 per 1,000) – that's an industry average of two per cent response. Your other costs were, say £5 for the product and approximately £3 for post and packing plus overheads (photocopier rental, rent, rates, lighting, heating, etc.) of about £5,000. You sold the product at £30, so you would take in £24,000 against costs of £22,600, giving you a net profit of £1,400. Not much, but actually a pretty good result from an approach to a list of prospects who didn't know you.

Now see what happens when you decide to re-mail those 800 customers who were pleased with your product. You offer a choice of a further product at the same price and a more expensive product, related to the one they bought at £60. Two and a half per cent buy the new product and a further two and a half per cent buy the more expensive product (because they have dealt with you before you will get a higher response to your mailing this time round), bringing in a total in further sales of £1,800. However, since your overheads have remained static, your expenses relating to these sales are only £660 (mailing 800 at 30p apiece, fulfilment of 20 items costing you £7 and 20 costing, say, £14). Your profits on this mailing are £1,140 so, while your turnover has increased by seven and a half per cent, the increase in your net profits is actually over 80 per cent.

This illustration, more than anything else, should show you the importance of back-end sales to the success of your business and the foolishness of the many business people who spend all their efforts selling cold to new prospects instead of cultivating a relationship with their existing customers.

As you focus on marketing to your best customers on a regular basis (and your less frequent buyers less often) you will be building on the most profitable formula known to direct marketing publishers.

Spin-offs

Never be content with single sales, always look for multiple sales and on-going relationships with your customers. This means that you need to develop or acquire a stream of new products. Where will they come from? One way to produce that stream of products is to use the spin-off technique. If you have a newsletter, publish collections of the best articles in book format. In my *Great Ideas* newsletter, for example, we have always run a mini-blueprint as a four-page centre-spread showing how to set up a particular mini-business – being a print agent, offering a gift basket service, pet and house sitting, a paper recycling business and so on. It was the work of half a day or less to assemble the best of these into camera-ready copy with a cover design and repackage them as a collection, *The Big Book of the Best Business Blueprints* – an ideal spin-off product that can be sold to new subscribers (who would like to catch up on past ideas we have published) or to new business opportunity seekers (to introduce them to the newsletter as potential subscribers) or to other existing customers who are not subscribers to the newsletter.

Other spin-off ideas could be a newsletter that follows up on a major information package you have sold on, say, small-scale property development or market gardening, or a series of products along the same lines as the first, but exploring different areas. If your first information product was a guide to understanding your computer you could follow up with spin-off products on making money with your computer, computer careers, a software tutor, running a dating agency using your computer, desk-top publishing and so on.

Through time you will build relationships with other specialist publishers who may have products that you can sell to your existing customers on a dropship basis (you do the marketing, take the order then send the other publisher the agreed wholesale price – usually 50 per cent – and they post the item to your customer). You may find that you can build good reciprocal business where the other publisher also sells your products on dropship. This is a cost-free way to extend your range of back-end products and enables you to build a good list of publications without the time and development cost of having to write them or commission them from other writers.

Branding

Ultimately, what you are working towards is developing a brand for your products so that your customers and others who see your promotional material will begin to associate your business with a branded range of information products or publications in a particular area of expertise, be it travel, business or whatever. Within the limited market that I operate in, my publishing enterprise has become known as a publisher of small business and career change publications of quality and integrity. Branding will help sales and help put your company in the forefront of its field, making your marketing easier and more effective.

Guarantees

Part of that branding will relate to how you deal with customer dissatisfaction and, if you are selling by mail order, that has to be part of the offer that persuades people that it is safe to do business with you. It is best to offer a full money-back guarantee on any product you sell through an advertisement or by direct mail and make it clear that it is an *unconditional* guarantee. A number of less scrupulous mail order publishers, especially in the business opportunity market, offer conditional guarantees that turn out to be worthless. These turn on the small print which says that a refund is only obtainable if the instructions in the publication have been followed exactly and proof is supplied that this has been the case. If the publication gives details of how to run a particular business it is unlikely that anyone who has tried it unsuccessfully will continue to complete the plan as outlined in the publication, running up further losses in the process just to be able to claim back the money they have paid for the guide. Other dishonest operators simply don't honour their guarantees and seem to manage to continue in business fleecing others, despite flouting the laws and regulations covering the mail order business.

Your guarantee must be part of your integrity and brand, with refunds given promptly and cheerfully so that the customer feels that it is both safe and pleasurable to deal with you again. Provided that you are producing quality publications that fulfil the promises you make about them, you will not find that you have an undue number of returns – possibly about one and a half to two per cent.

Cutting costs

A penny saved is a penny earned, says the old saw, and, while the kind of penny pinching that results in poor quality and shoddy presentation is counter-productive, it makes sense to keep your expenses lean and avoid wasting money that could be used more profitably. Some suggestions that may be helpful in keeping your costs under control are:

- Use a two-step process in advertising and mailing – a classified advertisement or a single sheet flyer mailed out to attract a response for more information so that your more expensive full information pack or brochure only goes to those with an expressed interest.

- Ask enquirers for a stamped addressed envelope not just because it meets some of your promotional costs, but because it qualifies the enquirer as serious.

- A variation of this is to ask for a 'no-risk goodwill deposit' for an initial report or information pack, redeemable against purchase of the publication being promoted or on return of the pack. Few people return the pack and ask for their money back and, while it may result in fewer enquiries, they will be more serious and worthwhile enquiries.

- Shop around for printing – it is an area where vast differences exist in prices for the same quality of work.
- Invest as little as possible in holding stock – work towards a production-on-demand set-up.
- Make sure that you are buying your supplies and other necessary purchases as economically as possible.
- When buying mailing lists pay more to get quality lists – lists of recent *buyers* of similar products to the one you are promoting.
- Look at ways of gaining no-cost/low-cost promotion – shared mailings (which you control and cost you virtually nothing), press releases, reader offers, etc.
- Consider other forms of joint venture marketing – finding other mail order publishers who can sell your publications on commission, getting your publications sold by related businesses, for example, a guide to market gardening sold in a garden products catalogue and so on.

9 | LEGAL MATTERS

Do you need a lawyer?

Boring and incomprehensible as the law might be to non-lawyers, there are nonetheless a number of important areas where you need to be aware of legal and other requirements in your role as a publisher. Most books on business tend to include lawyers among the list of professional advisers that it is advisable to retain, but to be quite honest you are unlikely to need to use the services of a solicitor anything like as often as you will be using your accountant's services or calling on help from your bankers.

My own experience is that over a period of nearly 20 years as a small publisher I have only needed legal advice or services about three times. On one of those occasions I had some excellent free advice from the Society of Authors, of which I was a member at the time, which saved me from a potential libel case and on the other occasions I had a brief consultation with a local solicitor who was a neighbour and didn't charge me for what amounted to no more than half an hour of his time in all.

Provided that you are sensible and observe some common-sense guidelines your experience should not differ greatly. Some of the areas you need to be aware of are briefly outlined in this chapter.

Bear in mind too that in the UK you can get a free half-hour initial consultation with a solicitor through the Law Society's 'Lawyers for Your Business' scheme. For details and a list of participating solicitors in your area ring 0207 405 9075. Readers outside the UK may well find similar schemes in operation in their own countries.

Copyright

The important aspects of copyright law in the UK are relatively simple, summed up in the notion that copyright in a written work belongs intrinsically to the writer from the moment it is set down on paper or in some other format and lasts under the Berne Convention for 'the life of the author plus 70 years'. Those rights can be transferred outright to others, such as publishers, for a financial or other consideration, but traditionally copyright is retained by the writer who hands over certain publishing rights to the publisher. In the case of a book or similar substantial publication, that broadly consists of a licence to print and publish the work exclusively, either solely in the home country, or throughout the world or in limited territories, for the period of the copyright agreement and any extensions or renewals of that contract. Again, readers outside the UK should investigate the copyright laws which apply to them.

Royalties

This agreement generally gives the publisher the right to decide how the work will be presented, illustrated, bound and marketed, the expense of such being entirely the publisher's. In return for the considerations granted by the writer, the publishers agree to pay the writer either a flat fee (rare) or a royalty arrangement of anything between five and ten per cent. This will usually be on the basis of the publisher's net receipts rather than on the sale price (which used to be the case) and there is often provision for an advance to be paid as a lump sum either on signing of the contract or on delivery of the manuscript, or sometimes a staged payment which splits the agreed advance between those two events. No further royalties are paid until that advance payment has been earned through copies sold

Clearly, as a small publisher, you can elect to follow the general practice among publishers as outlined above, though you need to negotiate a more flexible arrangement with your authors. You may decide to offer a higher royalty in lieu of an advance payment and, as your product may also be selling at a higher price than ordinary hardback or softback books in the shops, the resultant payment may be considerably more than the writer would get for each individual sale of his or her work from a conventional publisher.

An example might be the offer of a modest £100 on agreeing the contract, a further £100 on delivery of the text and then a 10 per cent royalty on the retail price of every copy sold right from the first copy. This may sound niggardly, but, in fact, it may be just as favourable to the writer, if not more so, than a conventional contract from a mainstream publisher.

If, for example, the conventional publisher offers a £1,000 advance and a 10 per cent royalty on net receipts and then sells 4,000 copies of a paperback book producing an income to the publisher of, say, half the retail price of £10, the total royalties payable will amount to £2,000, perhaps over a period of two to four years.

By contrast, the small publisher may sell, over that same period, some 500 copies of the work in a substantial ring-bound format retailing at £49, paying a royalty of £4.90 per copy. With the two small advance payments suggested earlier, the writer would earn a total of £2,650.

Contracts

Your contract with authors could be a simple letter outlining in broad terms what is agreed between you, or it could be modelled on the more complex legal documents used by most publishers. I would recommend that you model your contract on the Minimum Terms Agreement developed by the Writers Guild and the Society of Authors which a considerable number of major publishers have adopted. This is a royalty-based agreement and encompasses such important issues as subsidiary rights (publishing of the work abroad, in other media such as film, television, electronic media, etc., over which both you and your authors should be clear). Once you have worked out a broad draft of what you want the basis of your contract to be, it might be advisable to ask a suitably experienced solicitor to cast an eye over it to see if you have left any obvious loopholes or ambiguities in it or omitted something that ought to be included. Once you have that basic contract you will be able to change and amend the small details, amounts, percentages and so on as you please. For readers outside the UK, contact your own equivalent of the Writers Guild.

Subsidiary rights

Do bear in mind, if drawing up your own basic agreement or contract, that subsidiary rights can be extremely valuable. You may not plan to attend the Frankfurt Book Fair, the publishers' big event where rights are sold and deals are done, but one of your publications may come into the hands of someone on the other side of the world who wants to publish it. If you have not covered the subsidiary rights in your agreement you may miss out on a valuable revenue stream that goes, instead, entirely to the author.

You may say, 'Good luck to her!' but since you are in business to make money and it is your publishing efforts that have caused the work to be shown to the world, you deserve some of the rewards that come from subsidiary rights, which are often split 50/50 with the author. Bearing in mind the size of the US market, for example, such rights can be considerable, perhaps netting more than the total profits from the home sales of the work – all for not much more than signing a contract and supplying the text of the book!

Further considerations

You must also safeguard yourself from the author's understandable desire to milk their work for all they can by including some restrictions on their being able to write or publish any similar work with another publisher whose book, produced and sold along conventional lines, could sweep your publication to the sidelines, unwanted and unprofitable. On the other hand, you should encourage your author to write linked or related articles for magazines and other outlets, as this will provide the best kind of publicity for the work itself.

Consider, too, the question of your future relationship with the author. While the Society of Authors is not at all keen on publishers tying their members into agreements on their subsequent books, as a publisher you can understand that the investment you have put into the author by publishing and promoting them through their book merits some payback in terms of loyalty and at least, perhaps, to the right of 'first refusal' on their next work.

Legal deposit copies

As part of the Copyright Acts publishers are obliged to send legal deposit copies of the books they publish to a number of designated libraries within one month of publication. One copy should be sent to The British Library in West Yorkshire (see end of chapter for address).

A further five copies for the Bodleian Library in Oxford, the University Library in Cambridge, the National Library of Scotland, the Library of Trinity College in Dublin and the National Library of Wales should be sent to the agent Mr A T Smail (see end of chpater for details).

Free books for you to publish

As copyright lasts for the author's life plus 70 years, this means that there is a huge body of work that is now out of copyright which you are at liberty to plunder for free material. Apart from classic literature (which many mainstream houses will be reprinting far more cheaply than you will be able to do) you may come across specialist works out of copyright which would have a sale to specific niche markets. For example, I have on my desk at the time of writing a flyer advertising, among other publications, a work entitled *The Science of Getting Rich* which was published in 1910, the author, the unknown Wallace D Wattles, having died shortly after publication. If the book turned out to have any merit there is no reason why I should not obtain a copy and publish my own version, the cost of acquisition and development of the title being limited to the purchase price of a copy of the book plus re-setting the type and other design elements. I could then sell this title as an electronic book on disk and print out single copies on demand from my computer, binding them with a simple hot-melt binder or presenting it in a ring binder. I could even give it away free as a premium gift.

There are many other possibilities for re-publishing such quality works – minority interest novels, Victorian studies of various kinds, classics of natural history, local history, etc. Remember, however, the basic rule of profitable publishing – find the affluent prospects before you find a product that you can sell! However, if you can acquire publishing rights for virtually nothing and your production costs are limited to scanning text into a word processor and re-formatting it, you can afford to offer a small range of specialist books at premium prices either printed out on demand or supplied on disk or through a specialist website and corner a profitable niche market.

Copyright Licensing Agreement

Protection from unauthorized use of copyright material has been addressed by the setting up in 1982 of the Copyright Licensing Agency (CLA) as a limited company whose aim is to protect the intellectual property rights of writers and publishers in their work. It issues licences to bodies such as schools, colleges and libraries for photocopying from books, magazines and journals and collects the fees from such copying, distributing these to the holders of the rights according to a formula based on statistical surveys and records of copying activity, distributing some £70 million since its inception. For further information contact: The Copyright Licensing Agency Ltd (see end of chapter for details). There are equivalent organizations in countries other than the UK.

Public Lending Right

Similarly, under the Public Lending Rights (PLR) system, public funds have been made available for writers, illustrators and some editors and compilers to be paid for the use of their work borrowed from public libraries. The payments made are proportionate to the borrowings of their books, based on a sampling exercise and, while this applies to writers more than to publishers, some publishers will also be their own authors and should ensure that they are registered appropriately to receive their share of the funds. More details can be obtained from PLR Office (see end of chapter for details).

Libel

The law of libel appears to be simple, but in reality, as they say, you don't want to go there! In English law there is a distinction between libel and slander, the broad distinction being that slander is a spoken defamation while a libel is where the defamation is committed to a more permanent form, usually written, but including drawings and recorded material such as film, radio and television. Broadly the main defence against libel is that the statements are justified or fair comment, though there are also defences of privilege, and offer of amends and apology, though the latter need not concern small publishers unduly. The main problem with libel from the point of view of the writers and publishers who may be subject to a civil action for damages, is that truth is rarely simple, often unprovable and likely to be judged by a jury. 'Fair comment', too, can be a minefield in such cases, as it is often difficult to distinguish the fine line between fact and opinion.

Libel is, for the most part, a concern for writers in the UK rather than for publishers since a new Act in 1996 amended the law with regard to the position of 'Innocent Disseminators' of a libel – publishers, retailers, internet service providers and other 'third parties', who, provided that they can show that they took reasonable care not to offend in the dissemination of a libel, have a measure of protection under the law.

Bearing in mind the kind of publishing that small-scale publishers are likely to be engaged in, few will have any real worries about potential libel actions, though it is useful to be aware of the general danger and take steps to avoid being in a position where a libel action might be taken up. It is, of course, possible to insure against libel proceedings. Contact insurance companies to see what was offer. Readers outside the UK should familiarize themselves with their own country's libel laws.

Obscenity

This is hopefully not an area that most small publishers are likely to be involved in. Nevertheless it is wise to have at least a rudimentary grasp of the dangers publishers may find themselves facing in this area. Obscenity is defined as that which is likely to 'to deprave and corrupt' those who read, see or hear it.

Blasphemy, sedition and incitement to racial hatred

In the UK, it is an offence to publish matter that may be seen as an incitement to insurrection, riot or civil commotion or to publish plays that may be seen to be threatening, abusive or insulting to racial minorities and likely to stir up hatred against them. Equally, while it is permitted to publish matters that may be seen to be anti-Christian, if they are considered to be 'so scurrilous and offensive as to pass the limit of decent controversy and to outrage any Christian feeling' the publisher may be prosecuted. This outmoded protection does not extend to other religions.

Imprinting, ISBNs and ISSNs

It is a legal requirement for published books to carry the publisher's imprint – name and address – inside. In addition books should be given an ISBN – an International Standard Book Number to be printed on the reverse (or 'verso') of the title page, while magazines, journals and periodicals should carry an ISSN – an International Standard Serials Number. These numbers identify the country of origin, the publisher and the title or edition.

The UK agency that assigns ISBNs and ISSNs is a department of J Whitaker & Sons Ltd, which also gives details of new publications in *The Bookseller*'s weekly list of new titles. This service is free of charge. For full information about ISBNs, ISSNs and listings contact the UK International Standard Book Numbering agency (details opposite).

Useful addresses

The Society of Authors, 84 Drayton Gardens, London SW10 9SB. Tel: 0207 373 6642. E-mail: authorsoc@writers.ord.uk

The Legal Deposit Office, The British Library, Boston Spa, Wetherby, West Yorkshire LS23 7BY.

Mr A T Smail, 100 Euston Street, London NW1 2HQ. Tel: 0207 388 5061.

The Copyright Licensing Agency Ltd, 90 Tottenham Court Road, London, W1P 0LP. Tel: 0207 631 5555. Fax: 0207 631 5500. E-mail: cla@cla.co.uk

PLR Office, Bayheath House, Prince Regent Street, Stockton-on-Tees TS18 1DF. Tel: 01642 604699. Fax: 01642 615641. Website: www.earl.org.uk/partners/plr/index.html

UK International Standard Book Numbering Agency, Woolmead House West, Bear Lane, Farnham, Surrey GU9 7LG. Tel: 01252 742590. Fax: 01252 742526. E-mail: isbn@whitaker.co.uk

Note: Readers in countries other than the UK should contact the equivalent organizations.

10 | THIRTY PROFITABLE PUBLISHING PROJECTS

1 Self-publishing

It is not uncommon for the drive to become a publisher to arise from the desire to see one's own work published. Given the huge number of eager would-be authors who have their work regularly rejected by mainstream publishers who, though publishing greater and greater numbers of books, are nonetheless faced with many times the number they can hope to publish, it is not surprising that many authors see their only hope of publishing to be in doing it themselves.

While it is a great ploy of vanity publishers to trumpet how many famous authors published their books privately (to persuade people to use their dubious services), conditions in most cases were very different, so while George Bernard Shaw, Benjamin Franklin and Rudyard Kipling are among those who have turned publisher for their own books, it is certainly not an easy way to fame or a guarantee of success – most of the famous self-publishers were already established and were cashing-in on their growing fame to get a bigger slice of the cake in a very different publishing era. Despite that, however, there are some encouraging stories from more recent times.

In the USA Judith Appelbaum began by self-publishing her book *How to Get Happily Published* before it was taken up by HarperCollins and sales have now topped 500,000. *The One Minute Manager* was self-published successfully at $15 by joint authors Ken Blanchard and Spencer Johnson against all the advice they received that the book couldn't sell at that price. They sold 20,000 in three months before selling the reprint rights to William Morrow. It has now sold 12 million copies. Similar stories can be told about best-selling author Deepak Chopra whose first book was published through a vanity publisher and his *101 Great Answers to the Toughest Interview Questions* is consistently in the top ten business books sold every month.

So – publish! Before you do so, however, consider how wide an appeal your book has, who will buy it and how you will reach them.

It is not for me to tell you what you should write about, but for your self-published book project to be profitable I would suggest it has to have some, if not most of the following:

- an interesting non-fiction subject
- a subject or angle interesting enough to get media coverage
- a definite group of potential buyers who must have and can afford the book
- an easy way of reaching them
- an economical production cost or format
- a high cost-to-retail price margin of at least 1:7 (e.g. production cost £2.50, selling price £17.50)
- the potential to sell well by mail order
- the potential to sell through outlets other than bookshops.

Of course you may successfully publish, promote and sell your book and be more successful than the majority of self-publishers who end up with a garage full of unsold books – and that may be all you desire, but to launch a successful publishing business you will need to follow on with other preferably related books or books by other writers to exploit your database of new customers. So, if the book you have written and subsequently published is about, say, the Scottish island of Arran, then think of following up by publishing books on other islands, or focusing on other angles on your island – *The Arran Cookbook*, *Climbing in Arran*, *Accommodation Guide to Arran*, *Arran Folk*, *The History of Arran*, *Walks on the Island of Arran*, *The Arran Literary Guide*, *Wildlife of Arran*, *The Arts in Arran*, *Arran Steamers*, *Photographs of Arran*, *The Arran Clearances*, *Eating out in Arran*, *Prehistoric Arran*, *Poetry of Arran*, *Arran's Future*, and so on. Such a series could be usefully branded by a good common design that will mark the books out, and they would sell in various locations on the island, throughout the west of Scotland and by mail order to Arran aficionados. I would guess that initial sales of such books would be in the 500–1,500 range with steady back-end sales year after year. The same formula could be applied to many places and most subjects.

If you are a multiple book writer or can see the possibility of your own work being just the start of a small publishing empire that will include the work of others, then go for it with enthusiasm tempered with caution. You will find a considerable amount of help from the following: The Author-Publisher Network and the National Small Press Centre. Details are at the end of this chapter

2 On-demand publishing

Whatever you decide to publish you would do well as a small publisher to focus on a project that operates on a publishing-on-demand system, that is, one in which your publications do not have to be printed up in the conventional way in hardback and paperback format, but are able to be produced in small quantities, preferably as single copies at modest enough cost to turn a decent profit. This, strictly speaking, is not a publishing project as such, but a strategy which you can apply to your publishing plans.

On-demand publishing can take a number of forms. At one end of the scale are complex machines costing thousands of pounds into which a computer disk containing the text of a book is inserted at one end which the machine can read, print off and bind a single copy and drop it out of the other end of the machine. That is certainly one of the models of the future for medium-sized publishers who will be able to publish as many low-demand books as they consider worthwhile.

The good news is that you can do the same on a more modest level by using the low-cost technology currently available. This involves, at a basic level, nothing other than a low-cost PC, some simple software, a laser printer and a simple form of binding.

Whatever your project you can publish it without holding stock, without expensive printing and without hassle. What is more you can publish literally hundreds of items, even as a small publishing house. All it takes is the preliminary work of putting them onto computer in the appropriate format.

The great beauty of publishing on demand is that as soon as you have text on disk you are ready to publish and can offer books to your market without worrying about whether or not they will be successful. Moreover, if you sell a few dozen copies you will still make a profit on that title. Three dozen copies of a title sold from a catalogue or list at $10 will make you a profit of around $300 – and if you were to achieve the same results with 100 titles then you would have the basis of a profitable business.

3 Local newsletters

Local newsletters are an excellent way for the tyro publisher to begin, though they are unlikely to become as profitable as specialist newsletters and magazines because of the limited circulation, low cover price and modest advertising rates that can be charged.

Village news-sheets

Local newsletters can either be based on a small local area such as a village or large housing estate as a community publication, or can address particular issues or interests within that or a larger community. The first might be monthly publication focused on a village, covering local events and activities, voluntary activities, local church and community programmes, news and events in the wider world that might affect the villagers and might also include contributions from various people in the village. Such newsletters or magazines are usually very welcome, helping to create a stronger sense of community. Since it is generally difficult to find local people willing to contribute time and energy to such a project on a long-term basis, it is more likely to succeed as a private publishing initiative, albeit one which encourages as much participation as others are prepared to offer from time to time.

Local interests

A newsletter focusing on particular local interests would have to cover a larger geographical area, as it would appeal only to those sharing that interest. This kind of newsletter, while benefiting from the sense of place that powers other local newsletters and magazines, would also share the characteristics of more specialist newsletters, requiring specific marketing rather than simply the setting up of an efficient distribution system, though there would be some scope for promotion through appropriate local interest groups who might share in the revenue from sales to their members.

4 Specialized newsletters and magazines

Newsletters are one of the simplest publishing projects and among the easiest to launch. It is not long since all you needed was a typewriter and a packet of duplicator stencils to launch your wisdom to the world. Now the basics are a home computer system, a DTP program and a cheap laser printer – and perhaps a photocopier if you are going to print your own small-scale newsletter. There are no entry barriers, but you still need a viable idea that will sell and you need to organize yourself for success.

Magazines are usually more complex, however, and the kind of magazine you are likely to be able to publish will be simple, aimed at a small niche market, as is a newsletter, and sold on subscription rather than on the news-stands.

Choose your topic

First, the idea – what is your newsletter going to be about? With the increasingly narrow focus in the magazine world the choice of your niche market will depend on finding an even narrower gap in the market. Your own knowledge, interests and enthusiasms may dictate your choice, but be careful of running with an enthusiasm which is not commercially viable. Do your market study: look carefully at what is available already by scanning the magazine racks and studying the titles available in *Willings Press Guide* which you should find in your local reference library. Ask around in the appropriate circles. Send a pre-launch 4-page sampler to selected prospects from your target group and ask them whether your idea is appealing enough for them to consider subscribing when it is launched.

If your interests lie, for example, in the field of computers, you may despair as you count the huge range of titles in the marketplace. If, however, you narrow your focus and combine two ideas you may come up with a newsletter idea that has possibilities. Is there a title covering computers in farming, for example? Could you combine two disciplines and come up with the *Schools Marketing Newsletter* or the *Bed & Breakfast Association News* for the thousands of people who offer B&B throughout the country who have no professional body or journal to support and help them?

Choose your style

Some newsletters are dull, boring things with little or no design – just the bare text flowing into single or double column pages broken up only by headings and sub-headings. Perhaps this is appropriate for people who want to read about things that we might find boring but are fascinating to them. However, there is no subject so boring that it cannot be improved by a well-designed newsletter with an interesting layout. Think of the kind of readers you want to attract and ask yourself what kind of newsletter style would be most appealing to them – something zany and witty, serious and dignified, a mixture of styles to suit the differing contents in the pages and so on.

Look at as many newsletters as possible and analyse what makes them good or bad in your view. If there is one you like, then use elements from that in the design of your own.

There is a correspondence course available in newsletter design from The Newsletter School; courses in various aspects of publishing, including newsletter design are available from the British Association of Industrial Editors and training in electronic design for publishing is available from PPA, See end of chapter for details.

Decide your marketing strategy

Well before you design, write and produce your first issue you will have to work out who your subscribers are likely to be, where they are and how they can be reached economically. Try to set down on paper a profile of your prospective readers: how old they are, which sex, what social class or occupations they are in, what newspapers they read, what their leisure habits are and so on. This will help you in making your pitch to them through adverts or sales letters and will give you an indication as to how you might reach them.

Can you make it pay?

Whatever you do, don't print up thousands of copies in anticipation of overwhelming demand – and do your sums first! Because of technology you can now launch a newsletter with extremely low print runs – in fact, you can almost do it on a 'publishing-on-demand' basis, printing out a single copy from your laser printer and stapling it together. This makes for the most primitive style of presentation, however, and it would be best to think in terms of having a small number printed cheaply, using the spares as sample back copies for those enquirers who insist on seeing the product first before buying or to send to the editors of magazines or journals who might give you free editorial coverage.

In setting your price you have to decide whether it is better to have more people paying less or fewer people subscribing but paying more. Do you want 5,000 subscribers paying £30, 2,000 paying £75 or 1,000 paying

£150? The best way to set your price is to run tests, sending the same mailing to three groups of prospects drawn from the same source in which the only variant is the price. A simple sum done on the results will indicate which is the most profitable option.

Where can you learn more?

How To Publish a Newsletter by Graham Jones (How To Books, ISBN 1 85703 043 5) is a comprehensive 176-page guide covering all aspects of newsletter publication by someone who has been a major producer and publisher of these for over 20 years and knows the business inside out.

Make $50,000 Per Year Publishing Your Own Newsletter by Dan Lee Dimke is an audio presentation nearly an hour long which is a guide to publishing your own newsletter for profit. You can order it (Ref. No: 523/18111) by credit card from Future World. See end of chapter for details.

Success in Newsletter Publishing: a Practical Guide by Frederick D Goss (The Newsletter Association). A very thorough and illuminating 271-page volume with a strong focus on profitability. Get details from The Newsletter Association (see end of chapter).

Publishing Your Own Specialist Magazine by Alan Greene (Kogan Page, ISBN 1 85091 979 8). This is a 'must read' if you plan to publish a magazine which is aimed at distribution on the news-stands and has a great deal of valuable information and guidance for smaller-scale publications too.

5 Business manuals and reports

There is a large market for business manuals and reports of the kind that might be described as 'money-making' guides. While there is a great deal of scam-filled rubbish published by a considerable number of dubious operators, there are also high quality information products in this field which supply guides and blueprints for running some very unusual businesses indeed, such as a guide to the little-known business of cleaning suspended ceilings – a business which can net a small business operator no less than £200 per hour, an average job taking some six hours (or three hours using two operators) with an invoice value of around £600 while the cost of the specialist cleaning chemicals used is only a few pounds with equipment costs to set up the business limited to below £100.

If you were looking for a business that is easy to learn, can be set up with minimal cost and can earn you as much as a bank manager, what would you pay for the information that could set you up in a business of this kind – information that is not readily available to track down in the public domain? £50? £100? £200? The information would be worth any of these prices, but the 46-page manual was actually sold for £39.95 – and sold well, being considered excellent value by those who bought it. To them, the information was priceless.

Provided the information you publish is seen to be of value by those who order it and it is information that is scarce or hard to come by, you can charge a reasonably high price for it. There are, on the other hand, a huge number of trite and relatively worthless reports that are sold and resold with reproduction and resale rights on disk or CD. Their existence does not invalidate the concept of highly priced, good value business information which people are happy to pay for.

Good quality business reports should focus on unusual or little-known businesses and business ideas that are not to be found in the books in mainstream publishers' catalogues. They should focus on the kind of businesses that take little capital and can be run, at least initially, from home and they should revolve around an idea or a concept that is unique or at least a little out of the usual. Typical subjects might be: *How to Set Up In Business as a Print Broker*; *Rent Second-hand TVs for Profit*; *Become a Car Importer*; *Run Your Own Discount Coupon Business*; *Profit from Government Auctions*, etc.

Business guides and manuals of this sort must give hard, practical information on how to set up and run a business generally, the specific requirements of the particular business enterprise covered, with information about techniques and 'insider secrets', sources of necessary equipment and supplies, marketing advice, and generally cover everything that someone who wants to run such a business needs to know. When you consider that such a blueprint could compare reasonably with the information and guidance provided by a franchise operation that might cost £15,000, paying between £30 and £100 for a complete blueprint to run a business doesn't seem untoward.

Where can you get such business information to sell? Clearly, if you have information or experience of specific businesses that could form the basis of the kind of report or manual discussed here, you could begin by putting it together as a business manual. If you are a writer or at least have fairly good writing skills, you can put together information through research or write up other people's business ideas into a saleable format. Since the kind of information you are interested in publishing is of a rather specialist kind, you could try a small classified ad in writers' magazines or in business opportunity publications along the lines of 'Business publisher seeks practical business ideas and plans for publication' or 'Writers of business manuals invited to submit ideas to business publisher'. You may be able to negotiate a flat rate with writers for the copyright to this kind of work, but, since you are unlikely to get anyone to write such a guide for less than £500, it may suit your cash flow better to pay them on a royalty basis.

Alternatively, you may find some existing information packages available on licence from other publishers or product developers which may still prove fresh enough to your clientele or to untouched segments of the market to be worthwhile. See end of chapter for details.

Another place that you can look for such publications, particularly e-books, is the internet. Try the following sites:

www.onlinepublisher.co.uk

www.informationsleuth.com/E-texts.htm

www.netbusinessmarketing.com

www.geometry.net/Computer/E-books.htm

Finally, the US Government has a vast quantity of copyright-free books, manuals and information of all kinds that is freely available for you to access, repackage and sell. For more information on this contact Owen Publications (see end of chapter for details).

6 Correspondence and study courses

Whatever your own area of knowledge or expertise, it could form the basis of a correspondence course or study course. Moreover, there are many experts who would be interested in collaborating with you in producing a range of such courses, which are among the most profitable forms of publishing.

A study course, as distinct from a correspondence course, is one where there is no necessary interaction between the purchaser and the supplier, whereas a correspondence course implies that there are set exercises accompanying each lesson which require the supervision or comment of a distance-tutor.

The kind of subjects that lend themselves to study and correspondence courses are varied, but all will have some practical skills, techniques or secrets that can be imparted in the chosen form, although a more sophisticated course might include visual or audio elements where these are more appropriate to the subject. A series of audio tapes might accompany a music course, for example, or a video might be included to show a particular set of actions or to take the student through a key process. Suitable study or correspondence course subjects related to employment skills or leisure pursuits might include:

Archaeology	Mending household appliances
Aromatherapy	Photography
Bonsai	Restoration of pictures and antiques
Book-keeping	Salesmanship
Collecting	Setting up a small business
Drawing and painting	Small boat navigation
Genealogy	Teaching skills
Home design	Trading stocks and shares
IT skills	Writing for publication

7 Part-work publishing

Part-work publishing is similar to study and correspondence courses, though, of course, there is no tuition element and, unlike a study course, there is no set structure or curriculum. Subjects can be those that are virtually never-ending, like studies of famous artists as produced by one major publisher many years ago. Each issue had a series of colour plates and black and white illustrations, the life story of the artist, critical appreciation of the work and so on. Other subjects could be classic cars, famous people, antiques, potted versions of works of literature, spiritual guidance, philosophy and psychology, science, astronomy, etc.

The key to a successful part-work programme is, as with most publishing programmes, to home in on an easily reached niche market and offer something that will appeal strongly to that market. A monthly series can be promoted using a standing order as the method of payment and, provided the monthly cost is seen to be relatively insignificant and good value is given with each monthly package, you could build a virtual income for life. You would only need 650 subscribers at $10 a month producing a gross income of $6,500 which could leave you with a net income, after production, post and packing and promotional costs, of around $40,000 a year.

Part-works can be produced as punched pages presented in a plastic envelope or folder or as A4 booklets and a substantial binder should be offered free with the subscription (always priced, but given free if the person subscribes within 10 days).

Part-works that go on for ever can be a meal ticket for life – and your client base can be sold other products for which your promotional costs are absolutely nothing.

8 Dropship agency

Dropshipping is an American practice which has entered the world of alternative or small-scale publishing and, while it is not actually a publishing project as such, it is a way of getting access to a large range of publications that you don't actually have to publish yourself. Essentially it is a way of expanding the titles you have available to sell and, in reverse, a way of selling more of your own publications.

Dropshipping is the system whereby a publisher's products are sold by another publisher or agent, usually as a back-end sale, the order being sent on to the original publisher with the agreed proportion of the price, and the original publisher of the work ships it to the customer. The usual arrangement is a 50/50 split, so that if the product retails at $16 plus P&P, the agent sends $8 plus the P&P amount received to the publisher who sends out the book. While the originator of the work gets only half the price of the book less production costs, he or she does not have to bear any marketing cost and, since this is often the most risky part of the operation, is satisfied, particularly if there are a number of agents, each selling a few copies regularly, as this can add up to a tidy sum with very little effort being involved.

The dropship arrangement on its own is no real basis for a healthy and profitable business, but once you have launched your publishing business you can build profits by (a) seeking agents to sell your book on a dropship arrangement and (b) seeking other publishers in related fields to your own and doing a deal to dropship their products as a back-end sale, made most effectively by putting the appropriate leaflet or flyer in with the orders you fulfil for your own book. At the same time try to negotiate a mutual dropship exchange in which the other publisher sells your information products as back-end sales to his or her customer list, an arrangement which will be mutually beneficial.

To link up with suitable publishers and agents try contacting other small publishers. The Independent Publishers Guild, The National Small Press Centre and Future World may be helpful, but many opportunities will present themselves if you keep your eyes open as you go about building your business and learning more about your particular field and publishing generally. See end of chapter for contact details.

9 Local guides

Local books and guides must be the area which has started off more small publishers than any other. Despite the plethora of small publishers focusing on such books, there is still plenty of scope here for new competition. It is a question of looking for gaps in the market and of establishing a brand reputation of quality.

The difficulty of publishing local books, which are bound to have fairly limited appeal and sales, is that they have to be priced to sell rather than at a price that would make them as profitable as a small publisher needs his or her books to be.

With the latest technological advances in print and book production small runs of local books are more viable and the secret is to multiply the possibilities as recommended in the first section of this chapter, either by covering a wide enough geographical area or by exploring and exploiting many more facets of the area's possibilities.

Bear in mind, too, that publishers can have more than one imprint and publish in different areas, so that a publisher could produce local material and, at the same time, be a publisher of, say, specialist medical books.

10 Local history

This is a similar, and similarly fertile, area for small publishing projects, as there is a growing interest in the history of the places we feel that we belong to. Local histories, too, lend themselves to extension by diversification into various aspects – general history of the location, industrial history, history of the great houses and estates, history of prominent people and so on.

A publisher could add to that rich seam by including reprints of old works on the area and by publishing facsimiles of historic documents – scrolls, magistrates' warrants, deeds, charters and so on – which would be of interest to many people, including tourists and overseas exiles as well as being of particular value to schools.

The secret of real success in this field of publishing, as well as many others, is the use of the imagination to come up with new information projects which might include text, facsimile documents, dramatized events on tape, maps and so on – a complete information kit of more interest and excitement than the production of yet another book to be crowded out of the shelves in local bookshops.

11 Town maps and trails

An extension of that thinking is to look more carefully at people's information needs, which are not always best served by books as such. Particularly in tourist towns and areas (and what areas are not tourist venues today?) what people need are 'quick fixes' – simple, cheap and easily graspable introductions to the main sights and aspects of a place.

When, as a publisher, you start thinking in terms other than books, you will begin to see the benefits and possibilities of other media which, though relatively cheap to produce, can be sold at a high margin and in considerable quantities.

Thus a visitor to a town or area will appreciate the need for a map of some kind to find his or her way around. How much more attractive the purchase of such a map will be if it also pinpoints the scenic beauties, the walks, the fine houses, museums, art galleries and other facilities and entertainments without the need to be continually switching between a map blowing in the wind and a book where it is not easy to find exactly what is being sought.

Give some thought, too, to the format of such publications. Perhaps what is needed is a town trail printed, perhaps, on a long folding card tracing a route easily followed by the instructions on each section of the card which also identifies the places and sights worth looking out for. By purchasing your easily handled, easily understood town trail the visitor will get exactly the right experience he or she is looking for.

12 Local eating/accommodation guides

This kind of local guide can be a much more attractive publishing proposition as it can be a cash-earner from both sides: it is a highly saleable item and it is also a highly desirable volume for local restaurateurs, hotels and other accommodation providers to be highlighted in by taking advertising space. What is more, as an annually updated publication, it is a perpetual money-maker.

Whatever format you decide on – hardback, perfect bound or saddle-stitched booklet – you must first decide whether your guide will be inclusive or selective. If selective, you will have to select by quality standards and operate some kind of rating system or you can be totally commercial and be selective by charging for entry into the guide. The latter approach is not one I recommend, not if you want your guide to have some standing and reputation as a reliable guide to a quality experience. If inclusive, your guide should be *totally* inclusive of all eating places and accommodation in the designated area. Where it becomes interesting is when you offer, as an addition to the lineage entry, the opportunity to buy additional space for owners to expound on the delights and specialities of their establishments.

The price of this advertising should relate to the circulation of the guide, which will be difficult to establish for the first edition, so you may have to offer a bargain price for the first year. Set prices for the various sizes of the adverts – full page, half page and quarter page – taking into account the total cost of printing.

13 Local entertainment guides

A similar operation can be set up to cover the entertainment and leisure aspects of a town or area, either on an annual handbook basis or as a regular monthly or quarterly publication. The same game plan should be followed of providing free listings, some editorial content and selling advertising space for entrants to set out their wares in greater detail. You may choose to produce your guide cheaply in newsprint, in full-colour glossy magazine style if the circulation is large enough to justify the cost involved, or settle for a basic booklet style, plain, simple but well designed.

14 Autobiographies

The old cliché that 'everyone has a book in them' means that there are a great many people writing their life experiences in the fond belief that what is fascinating to them will translate into a mountain of book sales. Sadly, this is seldom the case, yet it does not stop the flood of such reminiscences. As a publisher, how can you benefit from this? Provided that such works are reasonably well written and have something to say that will interest readers, it should be possible to produce and sell them in the limited quantities that modern technology makes economically viable. Thus an edition of between 100 and 500 copies can be produced in some format or other, funded by the author or in a joint venture so that they can be sold by the author to family, friends and neighbours and through local shops. Some can be given away by the author and there may be scope for sales through associations or groups that are linked in some way to the author.

While this might be regarded as vanity publishing of a sort, what is being recommended here is the provision of an honest book production service for those many authors of autobiographies who would be pleased to fund the publishing of their life stories on an appropriately modest scale rather than be fleeced for huge amounts of money by the vanity press. The important consideration here is that it must be made clear to the clientele the basis on which the service is offered and that there may be very few sales possible beyond what the author is capable of achieving from his or her own contacts. In some cases this may prove negligible, but you may be surprised how successful some will be in selling copies of their book to acquaintances, old comrades and others who have an interest in the playing field on which they have lived out their lives.

Once you have established a format for the series and have streamlined your production process you will find that it is possible to make £150–£300 per autobiography produced, so the production of one or two a week should not only be possible, but financially rewarding, bringing in an income of around £25,000 a year.

15 Family histories

Family histories are another area where the desire to explore the roots and history of one's family opens up a need for some kind of modest publication of the results for circulation within the family and those interested in it.

Again, depending on the required numbers of the publication, a variety of publishing formats can be developed to meet this need, from a photocopied or laser printed A4 volume hot-melt or comb bound to a proper paperback or hardback book in quantities of a couple of hundred or more. Clearly the kind of family history that is wide ranging and comprehensive and not just a study of a few generations of a small part of a family tree will have much greater sales potential. If such studies were of a general nature then a great many people with that name would be interested in having a copy of a book that detailed their origins and gave information about the family's place in history, outstanding family members and events and so on.

The potential of a catalogue built on a huge backlist could be tremendous, with thousands of Fitzwilliams and Johnsons and Perkins buying the volume that told them about their family heritage – and if these volumes were produced on a publish-on-demand system the series could be extremely profitable.

16 For sale/wanted/exchange lists

While it may be thought that this sort of function is well catered for in local newspapers, there is scope for the development of specialist list-based publications. Examples of these are newsletters like *Government Auction News*, lists of repossessed properties, collectors' periodicals, friendship and dating contact sheets and so on. It only requires the exercise of some imagination and the identifying of specific groups with needs and wants to create a niche market publication that could eventually become as successful as *PC Mart* or *Micro Mart*.

Once you have identified a potential niche, put together a simple first issue, produce a few copies on a photocopier and promote it by a few classified ads in appropriate magazines or send out a press release to get more general coverage and see whether your idea hits the jackpot. If it does, fine, if not, what have you lost? Put your thinking cap on again and come up with the next idea and keep trying until you succeed.

The main problem with this kind of publication is finding the content for your first issue. The answer is to approach a large number of people advertising in other places and offer them a free advert in your first couple of issues. Approach suppliers and traders with an offer of discounted adverts and, while your first issue will not be bulging with adverts, it will at least look like the start of something good for those interested in the area you have chosen.

17 Company newsletters and magazines

With the increasing emphasis on good communications, there is a growth in company magazines and newsletters both for the workforce and as external communications with customers and others. Many companies, however, do not have either the skilled staff or spare resources to produce such journals and will be happy to consider outsourcing them to a writing or publishing professional.

There are a number of approaches you could adopt. You could, for example, ask companies for a copy of their internal communications for a report you are writing on company publications. This will not be a lie, for, on receiving a number of such publications you could easily use them as the basis of a report on the style, writing, presentation and effectiveness of such communications, making sure that you say at least a few complimentary things about each company's publications before gently pointing out deficiencies, or where and how they could be improved. Your report could then conclude with an offer of free consultancy to any company seeking to improve its publications or this offer could be made separately in a personal letter to the MD.

During the free consultancy you would find out how the publications are produced and by whom, who writes the copy, what the objectives are, the editorial and production costs and, on the basis of the replies, you could then present proposals for improvement, including an offer to undertake the publishing function on their behalf, thus freeing up company resources and providing an objective external professionalism.

You will find this much easier than you think, as many companies have not properly considered what they are trying to achieve through their publications and will welcome a fresh view and a more objective and effective approach. You may find, for example, that a single page monthly or fortnightly news sheet will meet their internal needs to convey and share information with employees much better than the glossy, stilted item they currently produce and that their magazine for customers fails to promote the benefits of their products and services, concentrating on inessentials such as the company's long history, the changes in board and staff membership and so on. Under you this publication could become a valuable sales tool, building up relationships with the customer base focused on the value of the products or services to them.

There are a number of quite large publishing companies whose sole business is the production of magazines and newsletters for companies, so there is room for the small operator who can provide the same kind of service to smaller companies who could not afford the services of these larger publishers.

18 Company histories

Company histories are essentially a self-congratulatory self-indulgence beloved of managing directors and company owners who believe that their pride in their company and its achievement will be much appreciated by others who receive a copy of a giveaway volume. This volume will, by its very nature, be full of pictures and have a nice full-colour cover.

Who are you to dissuade them from this indulgence? While you recognize that such a volume will not improve sales figures, will not be read by anyone outside the company (and probably by few within), if a company's board want to sanction such a project for reasons of prestige and because they see a book as a giveaway that might enhance the sales literature and other marketing efforts of the company, it may as well be paying you to produce this rather than anyone else!

Clearly, the longer established a company is the more likely they are to want to trumpet their history in this way and, given that a hardback book, produced in quantities of, say, 5,000 copies, will cost them no more than £3–£5 to give away, it is seen to be a comparatively inexpensive promotional project. If you do the entire job of writing the book and having it printed, you could make as much as £10,000 from a substantial company history which, given that the company would be providing a great deal of written and archival material for you to work from, should be completed in around three months.

As with company newsletters and magazines, you will need a clear idea of what the company is aiming at in terms of the finished book. Who will be the readers? What story needs to be told? Who needs to appear in the book? Who has information? Who needs to be consulted? You could prepare a checklist of questions of that nature to create a brief for your writing.

19 Reprints

It was mentioned previously that the reprinting of out-of-copyright work was a source of free material for publishers. While this presents a wide open field for easy and low-cost publishing projects, what you must avoid is reprinting popular or classic works that are more effectively and more cheaply done by large and established publishers with the financial muscle and scale of operation to produce these easily and cheaply in an attractive form you could not hope to emulate at the price.

What you need to look for is a subject area where there are less popular out-of-copyright books, which are nonetheless wanted by collectors, and those interested in these subjects or areas. Minor novelists, obscure academic and historical works, works on magic or country matters might well be fruitful fields to examine. Clearly, you have to obtain at least one copy of the book you want to reprint. The text can then be scanned in to your computer with a scanner using OCR (Optical Character Recognition) software or each page can be photocopied to provide CRC (Camera Ready Copy) for printing either in traditional paperback or hardback format using a specialist short run printer, or in larger A4 format with a soft binding of some kind as discussed in Chapter 6. You might also, having captured the text via OCR scanning software, turn it into Rich Text Format and use these files to create an electronic book with all the marketing advantages that these have – no stock to hold, many titles ready to produce on demand and the ability to sell texts over the internet.

If considering a reprint publishing project, think carefully about the demand that may exist for various publications and how easy or difficult it will be to reach the audience. Is there enough demand for you to make a profit? Is there too much work involved for too little a return?

20 Directory publishing

You may consider directories to be the dullest of literary productions, but they can be very lucrative money-spinners (producing around five times the profits of general book publishing) and, while requiring a lot of initial work to create, are easy to update and can produce repeat sales year after year. There are directories of everything and everyone, but the secret is to find a new or unexploited niche or to find a new angle on existing directory categories.

It is also the case that of the two kinds of directories, consumer directories and business directories, the first are usually sold through bookshops, with all the problems that both authors and publishers are only too well aware of, while business directories are generally sold directly to users by mail order, which gives you control of the distribution and sales process.

A directory of websites has recently been published and, while that might be thought to be superfluous, it has nonetheless been welcomed by web surfers, as it is still hard to beat the book for convenient and easily accessed information. What else might be welcomed in the area of the new technologies? A directory of web designers, content providers, ISPs and related internet services? What about a directory of authors willing and experienced enough to write the words that every web page needs?

On a wider front, what about a directory of kennels and catteries? A directory of business opportunities? A directory of politicians detailing their particular interests and stances on the various matters people want to lobby them about? A directory of copywriters? A comprehensive directory of churches across the country? A directory of clowns and entertainers? It may be that the best approach is to look for a specialist segment of an existing market and to go for a very targeted directory. For example while there are many general bed and breakfast directories, you might decide that a directory of bed and breakfast establishments under a certain price might be an attractive buy, or that a directory of Christian bed and breakfast establishments would sell well to the appropriate clientele through religious and church publications.

Directories are either compiled or non-compiled, with most being compiled. In other words, some directories include every listing in the field (non-compiled), while compiled directories have entries on the basis of either editorial selection or invitation, and may involve varying degrees of recommendation and quality control. An example would be the Consumers' Association's publication, *The Good Bed and Breakfast Guide*, the only B&B guide, as far as I am aware, that you cannot buy your way into or be listed in other than by an independent recommendation followed by a quality control check by the guide's staff. Entry to most guides of this nature is also selective, but only by the fact that you pay for an entry, which means that the value to the purchaser is limited, since the most awful establishments will still appear in the book simply because they have paid for inclusion.

This illustrates why directories are very profitable, as they can gather money at both ends of the operation. The buyer clearly subscribes to or buys the publication, providing one revenue stream, while income is derived from the listings either by a charge for entry or the selling of additional space as advertisements. Some directories, of course, like some magazines, are controlled circulation publications – in other words they are distributed free to the end users and thus provide entrants with access to the whole of their primary market. A directory of wholesale craft suppliers could, for example, be distributed free to all craft shops in the county, region or country. In this case the whole revenue depends on the charge for entries or advertising. In general my advice would be to make your directory as comprehensive as possible by including all known listings in basic format and offer an enhanced entry and/or additional advertising space to build the revenue from this side of the operation.

Since a directory project is likely to rest on mail order sales, an essential starting point is whether there is a large enough mailing list of prospective buyers in existence or appropriate and effective advertising media that can form the basis of your sales campaign.

The way information in directories is handled is different from other books in that directories are reference works and it is generally helpful to show the information in different ways to help readers to access it. There will be a main entry, probably alphabetical, then shorter listings by area or town, by particular aspects of the product or service or characteristics of the entrants, or by any other category that searchers will be likely to use to find the information they need. This is where computer and database software can make the compilation of directories relatively easy, as the information can be extracted and presented in different ways with comparative ease.

The setting up of a directory will involve considerable editorial research with masses of mailings to prospective entrants inviting them to have an entry and/or additional advertising in your directory. Once you have built up a database of participants it will become easier to contact them for each new edition of the directory to update their entry. All this will have to be costed into the budget in addition to advertising and promotional costs to launch the directory and establish it as a 'must-have' item for those at whom it is directed. Likewise you will have to budget for the mailings to create sales, bearing in mind that you will only sell to a small percentage of those mailed. This percentage is, however, likely to be larger than that expected from a typical mailshot and you may find it to be as high as 10 to 30 per cent in contrast to the typical mailshot response of two to three per cent, depending on how the value of your directory is perceived.

Against your budget for costs, set down your anticipated revenue, being conservative rather than over-optimistic. Work out three different figures based on different anticipated returns to your sales mailshot and similarly work out different advertising revenue figures based on different percentages of the available advertising space for enhanced entry sales being taken up. This should give you a low, medium and high revenue estimate to set alongside your more carefully calculated expenditure estimate. You should at least break even on your low estimate, show a decent profit on your medium estimate and if you achieve your highest revenue estimate it will be time to break out the champagne.

For an in-depth treatment of directory publishing try to track down *Directory Publishing: A Practical Guide* by Russell A Perkins, ISBN 0 913061 01 8 published by Morgan-Rand Company.

21 Publishing service for authors

While not recommending that you set up a vanity press operation, there is certainly a demand for book production services for authors who lack the knowledge or experience in book production. Once you have gathered sufficient experience in this area yourself and know how to produce a decent book at reasonable cost, you could be helping others to get their work published, albeit with the warnings about the difficulties of selling the books once produced.

You could develop this service further by taking on clients with books in a particular subject area, which would enable you to put together a simple printed catalogue that could be distributed by the authors as well as yourself, so that all the authors help each other to promote the books.

Remember, too, that your publishing service could focus on non-traditional formats, such as A4 comb-bound manuals, e-books on disk and e-books sold on an internet site bearing your imprint. A number of sites of this kind already exist (see section on e-books later in this chapter).

You could also share with your clients some of the sales approaches and techniques that self-publishers have found to be effective, perhaps by producing a booklet or other guide to marketing and pointing them towards the following books:

Marketing for Small Publishers by Keith Smith, Inter-Action Imprint, ISBN 0 904571 34 3.

How to Market Books by Alison Baverstock, Kogan Page, ISBN 0 7494 0126 5.

22 Specialist monographs

An extension of this idea would be to publish very specialist monographs and technical papers of various kinds to meet the needs of highly technical or academic markets. Since academics rely on publication for recognition and advancement, a specialist publishing house producing, say, 50–100 copies of a work on a co-operative basis could become an esteemed and influential publishing house.

This kind of project is again made possible by the new publishing technologies and the innovative formats these permit. Such a project could operate on the basis of charging the author a fee based on costs plus a set profit element and splitting the copies 50/50, so that they had copies to sell and you would keep a stock for sale to produce further profits. The cost of these works would be relatively high, given the extremely limited market for such esoteric texts and the small volumes produced.

23 Poetry publishing

Poetry is always considered to be the unprofitable area of publishing, but it was immensely popular and profitable in the nineteenth century, with the great British public waiting with bated breath for the next volume of verse from the Poet Laureate, Alfred, Lord Tennyson, whose books sold in their tens of thousands, contrary to his grandfather's assertion on paying him ten shillings (50p) for an ode on his grandmother's death that it would be the only money he would earn from his poetry. In fact, the receipts from the first few months of sales from one poem, *Enoch Arden*, would have kept a schoolmaster or a clergyman for 50 years. Lord Byron, too, became rich overnight on the publication of Cantos I and II of *Childe Harold's Pilgrimage* in March 1812.

The world is not so kind to poets now, though the top poets still do well, with the late Ted Hughes topping the sales league with 172,174 books in 1998–99, Seamus Heaney coming second with 34,690. Once you drop below the top dozen poets, however, sales and income drop dramatically, with sales running at a couple of thousand, or even just a few hundred books, based on bookshop sales.

However, the picture is not as bleak as it appears, for, as one small publisher of poetry pointed out in a letter to a newspaper following the publication of a league table of sales in verse on 5 October 2000: 'It seems slightly contradictory to report that bookshops stock (and sell) very little poetry, and then produce sales figures based on bookshop sales. Like most small independent presses, the majority of our sales are now via mail order, author's readings and the internet.'

This is the clue to making some money from the publication of poetry: small editions in economical formats, mail order and, above all, the authors as sales agents meeting their public face to face. While no one is pretending that there is big money to be made in poetry publishing apart from the star poets, it should be possible to publish poetry at a profit. Here are some ideas for doing so.

Publish poem cards, poetry sheets and posters. These are cheap to produce, can be printed in small numbers and have a high mark-up. They also cost the buyer very little, so someone who might demur at paying out £5 or £10 for a book of poetry might well part with 50p for a more ephemeral item.

Instead of simply having a poem on a card for its own sake, create some poetry postcards. Design four cards using photographs, clip art or copyright free computer images to enhance the poems and lay them out on an A4 sheet, designing another sheet for the back of the postcards with the usual postcard layout of section for message, one for the address and a square for the stamp. Have these printed back-to-back on an A4 card, either in black and white, in sepia or in two colours and ask the printer to guillotine the card into the separate postcards. By having 500 printed you will end up with 2,000 postcards with four separate designs and poems which you can sell individually, in sets of four or in packets of 12 for people to use as postcards and notelets. The cost of each card should be no more than 3p–4p and each can be sold for 10p–15p, sufficient mark-up for retail distribution. If you were to do a series of such cards you could offer a package to the individual authors of having cards done in batches of four, charging them a fee to cover the cost in return for half the cards – both you and the author then stand to make around £100 each from the sale of the cards.

Another way to make poetry more saleable is to produce small volumes of the work of individual poets or anthologies of several poets' work and dedicate a part of the proceeds to a deserving charity or cause. This is a win-win-win situation for you, the poets and the charity concerned, as sales will be easy because people who might not otherwise buy and read poetry will buy a copy to support the cause. This formula could be enhanced by having the book sponsored by local advertisers, charging them enough to cover the production costs. With all the contributors and the supporters of the cause or charity selling books to friends, the volume should be a modest success at the least.

Think, too, of other guises in which you can sell poetry: printed on mugs or T-shirts; as bookmarks; on gift tokens (sell the idea to the companies who produce them); on disk; on an internet site; on business cards; on the outside of envelopes; on gift scrolls; iced onto cakes; on answering machines; on poetry walls in dentists' and doctors' waiting rooms. Think also of unusual ways to make poetry pay – writing birthday odes and wedding speeches in verse for a fee; by publicly displayed poems where people throw a coin into a receptacle if they have enjoyed the poem; by a poetry auction; poetry readings; poetic entertainment at functions and so on.

Recommended: *How to Publish Your Poetry* by Peter Finch, Alison & Busby.

24 Postcards, posters, greetings cards and other ephemera

Some of what has been said in the section above applies equally to non-poetry postcards, posters, greetings cards and other ephemera, but what needs to be emphasized here is the huge market for such ephemeral publications (though some of these, far from being ephemera, will become collectors' pieces).

The greetings card market comprises some 800 or so publishers, varying from huge printing and publishing conglomerates down to individuals drawing, designing, writing and sometimes even printing their own cards as well as selling them through the trade and at fairs and other venues.

While many artists will be able to obtain commissions from big card wholesalers who produce rapidly changing designs for sale through newsagents and other outlets, you are more likely to be interested in producing a small, upmarket range of quality cards sold into specialist card shops. The key here is to develop a distinctive style and approach that marks your cards out as new and attractive offerings in a fast-changing contemporary market, though anything too way-out may be counterproductive. The best-selling original cards tend towards warmth and simplicity.

Since designer cards are individual, you can start with just a handful of designs and build up to a wider range gradually as the first cards are successful. The same applies to postcards, posters and other card- and paper-based items. The latter might be mock certificates, humorous notices, reproductions of ancient documents, cut and stick models and so on. There is a high demand for such novelties as impulse buys and small gift purchases. Packaging these attractively and durably is important and there is scope for follow-on or back-end sales by including details of other items in the range and where these can be purchased directly.

What ideas can you come up with for saleable items in this area? Postcards of local views and attractions? Making postcards of hotels and other leisure attractions for the owners or operators to sell? Posters for exhibitions and shows that might be purchased as mementos? Cut-out models of local buildings or 3-D scenes of local events? Items celebrating local legends or history? Success is only limited by the limits of your imagination and creativity.

25 Teaching resources

Most publications tend to be aimed at the general public as a market, yet there is a huge and easily reached market in education, where there is a demand for teaching materials and resources to meet the needs of pupils and teachers.

Following the advice given earlier in this book, what would-be publishers should be doing is identifying an easily reached market with specific needs and then creating products to meet that need.

Teachers are an easy group to reach both through advertisements in professional journals and by direct mail, as there are several companies who can supply mailing lists of schools and other educational establishments identified by various categories such as type and size of school, by subject, by location and so on. What is more, some such companies operate a shared mailing into schools on a regular basis whereby a publisher can have a sheet inserted directed to, for example, the Head of Drama for a very modest amount, a great deal less than doing a direct mailing themselves and almost certainly as effective. Try Hamilton House Mailings (see end of chapter for details).

When thinking about tackling an educational publishing project, think on a wider basis than books, unless these are directed at the teacher or are designed (and priced) to be a photocopiable resource with worksheets, examples, self-study and self-assessment units and so on. Think, too, about producing kits on appropriate subjects which would include instruction sheets, items for simple experiments, facsimiles of original documents, learning games and role plays, etc. A well-thought-out kit of this kind could provide a teacher with material for a number of lessons or even a full term's work and this would be a very attractive feature, especially if the kit covered some essential aspects of the Curriculum.

If you do not have educational experience, you will find that there are many teachers who have developed some very imaginative lessons and worksheets for their own use who would be interested in having these published to share with others. It would be comparatively easy to find such authors simply by putting a small advert in an educational newspaper or sending out a press release to the educational press.

Having had success with one such pack it would be relatively easy to develop further packs in the same area with the advantage that many of the short-run, alternative technology production methods allow for small quantities of such publications to be made up on demand, so cutting losses from the inevitable overproduction that over-optimism can create.

26 Remaindered books

This is a publishing idea that takes advantage of other people's mistakes or left-overs and is a way of profiting easily and quickly from a specific activity that is part of the mainstream publishing world. The costs of this project are low and the potential profits are high, with almost no marketing costs.

Of course there are people who deal in remaindered books – books that publishers have withdrawn from their lists. These are sold off to specialist dealers for pennies and then sold by them either to retail outlets that sell cheap books or through a mail order, often half-price, catalogue. You will not be competing with them. In fact, you will be dependent on them for supplies.

This project is one that relies on targeted niche marketing. Here is how it works. First, get copies of the catalogues of several remaindered books dealers and identify books in these catalogues that have a specific appeal to a particular market served by a number of specialist magazines. The book might be, for example, on modifying and upgrading your home computer or a photography book on portraiture. You then contact the dealer and ask how many of the books they have and what price they can offer you if you were to buy the lot (you might be looking at anything between 50 and several hundred books). Assuming that you can do a satisfactory deal, you could buy say, 215 copies of a hardback book retailing at $15.95 (which was in the dealer's catalogue at $7.95) for around $375 ($1.75 per copy).

Your next step is to write in turn to the editors of several of the leading specialist magazines in that area telling them that you have limited numbers of a fine hardback book (give a full description) which normally sells at $15.95, and which you are prepared to offer to their readers at only $6.95, and enclose a copy for their perusal.

Assuming that this is an offer that the editor would like to make to his or her readers they will then make an announcement that these books are available from you at a specially negotiated price and, hopefully, orders will flow in, clearing your stock and giving you a mailing list of people who would be interested in further offers of that kind.

Why should the magazine editor give you what is effectively free advertising? Basically, because they want to be able to offer benefits to their readers that will cost them nothing and make their readers warmly disposed towards the magazine. In some cases you may have to offer a margin of the profits to the publication; however, that is infinitely preferable to having to pay sky-high advertising rates that you would not ordinarily be able to afford for such a low-margin project. When you find an editor willing to play ball, you stand to make nearly $700 clear profit on this easy project which you will have accomplished just by writing a few letters.

27 Personalized children's books

This is an increasingly popular publishing idea and there are a number of dealerships that provide you with the software and pre-printed pages of storybooks into which a child's name is inserted at appropriate places throughout the story, sometimes with additional details specific to their lives. Once printed, the pages are then bound in a special heat-sealed cover to provide a storybook in which the child appears in the starring role.

There is no reason why you should not create a similar enterprise yourself. All you need is a selection of stories typeset on your computer with scanned-in illustrations. You the insert the child's name and details on computer – a few minutes' work – then print out the pages on heavy, good quality paper using a suitably large font. The book is then bound in a hot-melt cover with plastic front, behind which is inserted an inkjet-printed front cover in full colour.

Such books could be sold through agents or retail outlets or by mail order with a relatively high price to cover the individual personalization and manufacture.

Dealership details are available from My Very Own Book and Personalised Book Company. See end of chapter for details.

28 Audio and video publishing

A broad outline of the technicalities of these publishing methods has been given in Chapter 6. What projects do these media lend themselves to? The growth in voice audio as distinct from music on tape is in the areas of self-improvement, instruction, and car entertainment of one kind and another. Bear in mind, too, that there are large numbers of people who are not readers but who have the capacity to listen to a tape in order to learn. Projects that could be successful might be: fiction on tape; 'how-to' subjects; tapes on self-confidence, relaxation, success strategies, career development and all kinds of general and popular subjects that might otherwise be presented in book format. You could launch your own 'College of the Car' series, producing a range of instructional and educational tapes for easy listening and learning while driving. Audio tapes are also excellent group learning aids and tapes could be produced for specific groups of people to gather and listen to – writers' circles, sales teams, retail staff, training groups, classroom learners and so on. Consider, too, the capacity of audio tapes to convey the sounds and atmosphere of places and events and special experiences, interviews, conversations and other voices – sounds which make for easier listening than simply hearing a voice talking at the listener.

Video projects, on the other hand, tap into a growing medium as people become more and more hooked on watching television. It is a medium of familiarity, a medium of choice and that makes it a very powerful publishing medium. Video has the same virtues as television: it's easy to watch, easy to absorb and easy to remember. It makes it an ideal learning medium and also has advantages over television, as it can be paused, rewound and rerun to catch or reinforce a process or a point.

Like audio tapes, the scope is endless and, once the master is created, copies can be made in relatively low numbers at low cost. Use video for projects where practical instruction or processes need to be shown. Think of the subjects that television has already laid the foundations for popular interest – gardening, DIY and home improvement, cookery and so on. Extend those educational programmes by creating your own instructional videos on choosing and serving wines, decorative techniques in the home, childcare, servicing your car, setting up your own business, managing your finances, laying out a new garden – the scope is literally endless.

Both video and audio tapes are ideal for recording important seminars and meetings, providing a readily saleable record of the event for participants and for those unable to attend but to whom the contents are of interest.

Think too, with both audio and video tapes, of producing an ongoing series or course in ten to twenty parts on a subscription basis, or a taped book of the month club to create a regular income from your publishing activities.

29 Telephone publishing

Publishing, in the twenty-first century, is to do with communicating information in forms and through media that people are comfortable with and the telephone is one such medium that is increasing in use and popularity because it is instant, direct and involves the warmth and personal contact of the human voice.

While the widest use of this medium using premium rate numbers is in the unsavoury area of 'adult entertainment' there are plenty of other applications for using telephone technology in publishing.

Some obvious ideas would be a recorded 'thought for the day'; information services that give a succinct summary of updated daily information on, for example, stocks and shares; horoscopes; racing tips;

training tips for particular professions; a telephone 'soap' diary; a recommendation service based on shopping tips; directories on line; dating services; an 'idea line', etc.

Linked to the idea of telephone publishing is a fax-back service, where reports and specialized information could be made available on premium rates. These services, and those involved in providing telephone advice and information on premium rate numbers, can be set up to run automatically and, with the right service, well promoted, can be very lucrative.

There are a number of companies in the UK operating premium number services and it is possible to start a telephone publishing business by using their services. One long-established company ABC 4 Telecoms Ltd, which has been established for a decade, offers free lines (i.e., there is no set-up charge, service charge or on-going rental). Once your service is set up they pay you 20p a minute where the calls cost 50p a minute, 30p a minute where calls cost 75p a minute and 50p a minute where calls are charged at £1 a minute (some of their share goes to BT as the prime provider). See end of chapter for contact details.

30 E-books and e-zines

Anything that can be published in traditional printed format can be published as an e-book or e-zine with the great advantage that after the origination costs have been met, production costs are minimal or zero, and delivery is considerably cheaper than printed matter if posted and no cost at all if delivered over the internet by autoresponder, e-mail or by issuing a password which enables the purchaser to download the publication as a file from a website.

While there are various levels of sophistication and technical expertise involved in e-book publishing anyone with average computer skills can launch it in its simplest format and gradually learn and acquire the more complex skills required for the more sophisticated options.

At its most basic, an e-book can simply consist of text-files loaded onto a floppy disk and sold by conventional means or advertised on a website, delivery being through the use of the postal system. The files can be as simple as Word for Windows® and read as such on screen or printed off, or you can use any of the proprietary e-book editing programs that are widely available.

The beauty of e-books, even at this simple level, is that once the book is complete on your computer, all you have to do is market it and make a copy on disk on receipt of an order, stick on an already created label and a simple cover for a more professional presentation, pop it in a board-backed or bubble-envelope and post it to your customer along with a flyer giving details of the other titles you have to offer.

If your e-book project is illustrated you may have to produce it as a CD-ROM to accommodate the size of the graphic files and make sure that you have the ability to produce one-off copies to meet orders. You will need a CD writer as part of your computer set-up for this.

You may find that you already have files on your computer that would provide enough material for your first e-book. My first e-book was a simple collection of my best small business articles which had been published in various small business magazines and it was given away as a free premium to enhance the subscription offer to my newsletter *Great Ideas*. Once I had obtained a copy of the simple editing program Writers Dream I soon had other titles on disk as alternative e-book versions of books I was publishing already in printed format, such as the *Escape Kit* for career-changing teachers. Soon I added the *Redundancy Report* and began to put other work into e-book format, including some copyright-free texts taken from the internet such as the classic copywriting text *Scientific Advertising* by Claude C Hopkins and other e-books which are made available by other 'infopreneurs'. Within a short amount of time I had a collection of a dozen or so e-books that could be sold as a complete collection, together with reproduction and resale rights.

Clearly, just as in any publishing venture, you should look for information areas that not only interest you but that are hot topics for a group of people whom you can reach comparatively easily. Remember, too, that your potential customers must have access to a computer. Be sure that you have the right to reproduce the material for sale if it is not your own.

Just as e-books can be uploaded to websites and downloaded by purchasers, so an e-zine can be put up on a website or sent by e-mail to those who have opted to join your subscription list. E-zines can be looked on either as free information which can carry sales material for other products in a disguised form, or as limited-access publications accessible by subscribers only. In either case, origination is virtually the only cost, as delivery over the internet either by bulk e-mail or via a free or password-protected website is pretty well cost-free. If you decide to charge for access to your e-zine it need not be high enough to discourage potential subscribers. What you need to aim at is a subscriber base (free or otherwise) in the thousands, so that many small payments will equal a good income (10,000 subscribers paying $5 a year means an income of $50,000 – almost all profit) or a small number of orders following the enticements offered in a free e-zine which will create the kind of profits you are looking for ($^{1}/_{2}$% of those 10,000 subscribers ordering one of your $90 products every month will mean an income of $54,000 less your minimal fulfilment costs).

You do not even need to have your own website in order to sell your e-book on the web as there are a number of e-book publishing sites operating that will handle your book and pay you on a royalty basis. Among these are:

Booklocker.com: an e-bookstore that pays 70 per cent royalties on a non-exclusive arrangement – you can still sell your book elsewhere. New submissions and guidelines from: http://www.booklocker.com/getpublished/published.html

Fatbrain at: http://www.ematter.com

E-booksonline (UK) Ltd ask for no setting up fee and pay 45 per cent royalties. Go to: http://www.e-booksonline.net

Eboox make no up-front charge and will list your e-book on their site for nothing, paying 50 per cent royalties six months in arrears. Go to: http://www.e-boox.co.uk

UK eBooks make a charge of £50 upwards for publishing your e-book but you get 100 per cent of the takings. Contact them at: http://www.uk-ebooks.com

SellYourBook.co.uk sells e-books for £3 and charges a £57 handling fee for hosting your book on their site, including maintenance and administration, paying 50 per cent royalties. Go to: http://www.sellyourbook.co.uk

Whatever the state of your computer knowledge it will become increasingly important for small publishers to come to grips with internet technology and be able, eventually, to offer downloadable e-books from a website. With a simple, but well-promoted website with a range of interesting e-publications accessible by credit card from a secure web page and delivered instantly by autoresponder as soon as the payment has been recorded, you will literally be able to make money while you sleep, with hardly any effort and at virtually no cost – the ideal business! What are you waiting for?

Useful addresses

The Author-Publisher Network, SKS, St Aldhelm, 20 Paul Street, Frome, Somerset BA11 1DX. Founded by John Dawes, the Network is a self-help organization for self-publishers, running courses and lectures and publishing a newsletter, *Write to Publish*. Membership is £25 a year.

The National Small Press Centre, BM Bozo, London WC1N 3XX. An organization offering help to small, independent and self-publishers through exhibitions, workshops and various publications, including a handbook. Annual subscription £15.

The Newsletter School, ASPECT, PO Box 43, Thatcham, Newbury, Berkshire RG13 4WH.

British Association of Industrial Editors, 3 Locks Yard, Sevenoaks, Kent TN13 1LT.

PPA, Silwood Park, Ascot, Berkshire SL5 4PW.

Future World, PO Box 153588, Irving, Texas 75015-3588, USA. Tel: 001 972 399 8400 (or Freephone 0800 96 0379). Fax: 001 972 399 8300. E-mail: sales@future-world.com. An excellent source of a huge range of books, tapes and CD-ROMS which provides a full-colour catalogue and a personalized website giving a 50 per cent dropship commission, up to 80 per cent wholesale prices and other benefits.

The Newsletter Association, Colorado Building, Suite 700, 1341 G Street NW, Washington, DC 20005

The Independent Publishers Guild, 4 Middle Street, Great Gransden, Sandy, Bedfordshire SG19 3AD. Tel: 01767 677753. Fax: 01767 677069.

The National Small Press Centre, BM BOZO, London WC1N 3XX.

Hamilton House Mailings Ltd, Earlstrees Court, Corby, Northamptonshire NN17 4HH. Tel: 01536 399000. Fax: 01536 399012. E-mail: HHMailing@aol.com

My Very Own Book, 33 Bridle Road, Burton Joyce, Nottingham NG14 5FS. Tel: 0115 931 3099. Fax: 0115 931 3308.

Personalised Book Company (UK), 2 The Grove, Mount Street, Diss, Norfolk IP22 3QQ. Tel: 01379 641444. Fax: 01379 641444. E-mail: sales@bestbook.co.uk. Website: www.bestbook.co.uk

Business manuals and reports

Avril Harper, Meander Press, Avallan, High Hesleden, Hartlepool, Cleveland TS27 4PZ. Tel: 01429 836865. Fax: 01429 837787. E-mail: avallan@aol.com

Business Opportunity Bureau, Greenlands, New Waltham, Grimsby, East Lincolnshire DN36 4YE. Tel/Fax: 01472 315834. E-mail: bromleyart@aol.com

Business Innovations Research, Tregeraint House, Zennor, St Ives, Cornwall, TR26 3DB. Tel/Fax: 01736 797061. E-mail: great-ideas@ukgateway.net

Owen Publications, Drawer 10, Battle Ground, WA 98604-0010 Tel: 001 360 887 8646 or go to: http://www.ipns.com/mailmaxx/govpub.htm

Telephone publishing

ABC 4 Telecoms Ltd, Paramount House, Branston Court, Branston Street, Hockley, Birmingham B18 6BA. Tel: 07005 301 000. Fax: 07005 301 001. E-mail: mailorder@pantherleisure.demon.co.uk

Premier Voicemail (provide premium-rate numbers, fax back and other services). Tel: 020 8236 0236. Website: www.premiervoicemail.co.uk

Keylinecomms (provide voicemail, premium and chat lines). Tel: 0870 124 0870. E-mail: Info@Keylinecomms.co.uk; Website: www.keylinecom.com

Suggested reading

How To Publish Yourself, by Peter Finch, Allison & Busby, 3rd edition, 1997

PPA, Silwood Park, Ascot, Berkshire SL5 4PW

11 | RESOURCES

This book has been able to give only an outline of the publishing process, covering a wide range of activities from traditional book, magazine and newsletter publishing to small-scale, home-based, internet and electronic book publishing plus some communication media that are not normally regarded as publishing in the strict sense of the word.

It follows from this that such a volume cannot be comprehensive and I have not pretended that what lies within these pages is all that you need to know to become a publisher. Far from it!

The best teacher, as with most human endeavours, is experience and I hope that this book will have provided a platform of ideas and knowledge that will at least be a good starting point for that experience to build on.

This chapter is intended to provide some guidance as to sources of further information, resources that will be useful to the new publisher and further reading to continue the learning process in greater depth on specific aspects of publishing. And because of the vast range of resources, this chapter is generally UK-focused. However, readers in countries outside the UK should be able to find similar resources in their own countries, using the material in this chapter as a guide and starting point.

Unless you intend to carve out a career in one of the large publishing houses (or even in a more modestly sized one) you will not need to study for any formal qualification and you are more likely to acquire your new knowledge about publishing on the basis of need. This will, naturally, leave you ignorant of a great deal of information and expertise that more formal and established publishers will deplore, but as an ex-adult education professional it seems to me to be the most practical basis on which to acquire skills in a new area. Once your level of ignorance gets in your way you will be motivated to learn whatever it is that you need to know to go on to the next skill level you need to accomplish your aims. It is the natural way that human beings have been learning successfully for many thousands of years. Do you really need to know about the intricacies of ems and leading? Why should you need to acquire skills in HTML when you can build a web page using a perfectly satisfactory proprietary program that does all you want it to do? What is the point of knowing how to do colour separations when your plan is to publish a simple single-colour newsletter? Learn what you need to learn as you need to know and use it.

Where to learn more

While you will learn a great deal from experience, from trial and error and from contacts with other publishers, both professional and amateur, there are courses available covering a wide range of key publishing topics and skills. Most of these, however, are designed for career publishers working in mainstream publishing companies and may not meet the more eclectic needs of the small publisher setting up on his or her own with little or no publishing industry experience. Look out for more specific localized courses in your local college or other institution focusing on, for example, DTP, building websites and other related or useful topics. In addition, there are a number of organizations that are extremely useful to the new publisher, not least in the personal contacts that are made between members. Full details of these are given here for ease of reference, as are details of useful books, even if some of them have already been listed earlier in the appropriate chapters.

Courses

The London College of Printing, School of Media, 10 Back Hill, Clerkenwell, London EC1 5EN. Tel: 020 7514 6500. Fax: 020 7514 6848. E-mail: t.bodenham@lcpdlt.Inst.ac.uk Website: www.lcp.linst.ac.uk
Offers a range of specialist postgraduate courses which lead directly into careers in professional publishing.

The Publishing Training Centre produces a number of excellent study courses, including a two-day course in picture research, Nicola Harris's detailed course on *Basic Editing* which comes in two volumes, one being the text of the course and the second being a book of practical exercises, including an assessment form. Contact: The Publishing Training Centre at Book House, 45 East Hill, London SW18 2QZ. Tel: 020 8874 2718/4608. Fax: 020 8870 8985. E-mail: publishing.training@bookhouse.co.uk. Website: www.train4publishing.co.uk

The London School of Publishing and PR runs a number of NUJ-approved courses, including *Picture Research*. Contact: The London School of Publishing and PR, David Game House, 69 Notting Hill Gate, London W11 3JS. Tel: 020 7221 3399. Fax: 020 7243 1730. E-mail: lsp@easynet.co.uk

Periodicals Training Council, Queen's House, 55–56 Lincoln's Inn Fields, London WC2A 3LJ. Tel: 020 7404 4168. Fax: 020 7404 4167. E-mail: training@ppa.co.uk

Training in Indexing is an open learning course offered by the Society of Indexers. Contact: Wendy Burrow, Society of Indexers, Globe Centre, Penistone Road, Sheffield S6 3AE. Tel: 0114 281 3060. E-mail: admin@socind.demon.co.uk

The Mega Strategy by Dan Lee Dimke, Future World, ISBN 0 86594 037 1. This is a complete course on home-based mail order publishing consisting of a book of 148 pages and four extended play audiotapes. Obtainable from: Future World, Dept 18111, Post Office Box 153588, Irving, Texas 75015-3588, USA. Freephone order line 0800 960379.

The Nuts and Bolts of Selling Information by Mail is a free course delivered as an e-book (or you can request a printed copy) from: Meander Press, Avallan, High Hesleden, Hartlepool, Cleveland TS27 4PZ. Tel: 01429 836865. Fax: 01429 837787. E-mail: avallan@aol.com

The Home Publishing Revolution is a massive practical study course provided in printed form in a ring binder or downloadable from a private website. Buyers have automatic dropship rights on buying the course. For a free information pack contact: PhilDee Ltd, (Dept No 1661), 2 Hilton Road, Disley, Cheshire, SK12 2JU. Fax (with Dept No) to: 01663 766063 or e-mail (also with Dept No): hpagent@phildee.u-net.com

Organizations

The Institute of Publishing, 78 Manor Way, Guildford, Surrey GU2 7RR. Tel: 020 7233 0935. Fax: 020 7233 0940. E-mail: tim@osceng.co.uk. Website: www.instpublishing.org.uk
Launched in March 2000, the Institute of Publishing covers the needs and interests of individuals working in all sectors of the publishing industry, including books, journals, magazines, newsletters, technical publications, newspapers, websites and on-line services.

Association of Little Presses, 25 St Benedict's Close, Church Lane, London, SW17 9NX. E-mail: asslp@geocities.com Website: www.geocities.com/Athens/Oracle/7911

The Society of Young Publishers is an organization which claims that 'you're never too old to be a young publisher'. The society runs meetings and social events and provides career advice to members. Contact: Diane Banks on 020 7873 6158. Website: www.thesyp.demon.co.uk

APE (Advice to Publishers and Editors) is an organization that runs an annual exhibition with low-cost seminars and free advice for those engaged in producing magazines, journals and newspapers. Contact: Lyn Porter, Exhibition Organizer, APE Exhibition Organizers, The Arcade Chambers, The Arcade, Aldershot, Hampshire GU11 1EE. Tel: 01252 357004. Fax: 01252 357001. E-mail: ape@nwh.co.uk; Website: www.apeexhibition.com

Association of Publishing Agencies, Queen's House, 55–56 Lincoln's Inn Fields, London, WC2A 3LJ. Tel: 020 7404 4167. Fax: 020 7404 4166. E-mail: hilary@apa.co.uk; Website: www.apa.co.uk

The Booksellers Association of Great Britain and Ireland, 272 Vauxhall Bridge Road, London SW1V 1BA. Tel: 0207 834 5577. Fax: 0207 834 8812. E-mail: 100437.2261@compuserve.com.

The British Copyright Council, Copyright House, 29–33 Berners Street, London W1P 4AA. Tel: 01986 788 122. Fax: 01986 788 847. E-mail: copyright@bbc2.demon.co.uk
The Council's aim is the protection of copyright in a worldwide context.

The Copyright Licensing Agency Ltd (CLA), 90 Tottenham Court Road, London W1P 0LP. Tel: 020 7631 5555. Fax: 020 7631 5500. E-mail: cla@cla.co.uk Website: www.cla.co.uk
The Agency administers and collects photocopying royalties on behalf of writers and publishers.

Directory and Database Publishers Association. A professional association for those involved in this area of publishing. Contact: Rosemary Pettit, Directory and Database Publishers Association, PO Box 23034, London W11 2WZ. Tel: 020 8846 9707.

Society of Editors. This society represents a group of 400 editors in all areas of publishing. Contact: Bob Satchwell, Society of Editors, The University Centre, Granta Place, Mill Lane, Cambridge CB2 1RU. Tel: 01223 304080. Fax: 01223 304090. E-mail: society@ukeditors.com

Society of Freelance Editors and Proofreaders, Mermaid House, Mermaid Court, London SE1 1HR. Tel: 020 7403 5141. E-mail: admin@sfep.org.uk Website: www.sfep.org.uk
Provides a range of services for members including training courses, conferences and a newsletter.

British Association of Magazine Editors, c/o Gill Branston and Associates, 137 Hale Lane, Edgware, Middlesex HA8 9QP. Tel: 020 8906 4664. Fax: 020 8959 2137. E-mail: bsme@cix.compulink.co.uk

Periodical Publishers Association, Queen's House, 28 Kingsway, London, WC2B 6JR. Tel: 020 7404 4166. Fax: 020 7404 6167. E-mail: info1@ppa.co.uk

INK, 170 Portobello Road, London W11 2EB. Tel: 020 7221 8137.
Trade association for alternative periodicals.

The Greeting Card Association, 41 Links Drive, Elstree, Hertfordshire WD6 3PP. Tel/Fax: 020 8236 0024.
Publishes *Greetings* magazine.

The Association of Learned and Professional Society Publishers. Contact: Sally Morris, Secretary General, The Association of Learned and Professional Society Publishers, South House, The Street, Clapham, Worthing, West Sussex BN13 3UU. Tel: 01903 871686. Fax: 01903 871286. E-mail: alpsp@morrisassocs.demon.co.uk; Website: www.alpsp.org

The National Small Press Centre. An organization for small and self-publishers which runs exhibitions, talks, courses, fairs, conferences and workshops. Contact: John Nicholson, Director, The National Small Press Centre, BM BOZO, London WC1N 3XX.

The National Poetry Foundation provides free information, and advice on poetry publishing and a magazine in return for a small membership fee. Contact: The National Poetry Foundation, 27 Mill Road, Fareham, Hampshire PO16 0TH. Tel: 01329 822218.

The Independent Publishers Guild, 4 Middle Street, Great Gransden, Sandy, Bedfordshire SG19 3AD. Tel: 01767 677753. Fax: 01767 677069. The Guild provides a forum for members to exchange views and information about publishing.

Publishers Licensing Society Ltd, (PLS), 5 Dryden Street, London WC2E 9NW. Tel: 020 7829 8486. Fax: 020 7829 8488.
The PLS represents the interests of publishers with regard to licences that permit photocopying of published works and disburses the money collected to publishers.

The Publishers Publicity Circle helps all book publicists to share ideas and information and their meetings provide a forum for the press to meet and find out about new books. Contact: Christina Thomas, Secretary, 48 Crabtree Lane, London, SW6 6LW. Tel/Fax: 020 7385 3708. E-mail: ppc-@lineone.net

The Federation of Worker Writers and Community Publishers promotes working-class writing and publishing. Contact: The Federation of Worker Writers and Community Publishers, Box 540, Burslem, Stoke-on-Trent, Staffordshire ST6 6DR. Tel/Fax: 01782 822327. E-mail: fwwcp@cwcom.net; Website: www.fwwcp.mcmail.com

UK Newsletter Association, Premier House, 11 Marlborough Place, Brighton BN1 1UB. Tel/Fax: 01273 682733. E-mail: ukna@btinternet.com

Electronic Media Round Table, 26 Rosebery Avenue, London EC1R 4SX. Tel: 020 7837 3345. Fax: 020 7837 8901. E-mail: esp@espltd.demon.co.uk

Books

The Small Publisher, by Audrey and Philip Ward, Oleander Press, ISBN 0 900891 59 9

Publishing and Printing at Home, by Roy Lewis and John B Easson, David & Charles, ISBN 0 7153 8510 0

How To Publish a Newsletter, by Graham Jones, How To Books, ISBN 1 85703 043 5

Success in Newsletter Publishing, a Practical Guide, by Frederick D Goss, The Newsletter Association, ISBN 0 9610222 0 5

Publish Your Own Specialist Magazine, by Alan Greene, Kogan Page, ISBN 1 85091 979 8

Design for Desktop Publishing, by John Miles, Gordon Fraser Gallery, ISBN 0 86092 096 8

The House Journal Handbook, by Peter C Jackson, The Industrial Society, ISBN 0 85290 135 6

Great Pages, by Jan V White, Serif Publishing, ISBN 1 878567 01 2

Directory of Book Publishers, Distributors and Wholesalers, 272 Vauxhall Bridge Road, London SW1V 1BA. Tel: 020 7834 5477. Fax: 020 7834 8812. E-mail: 100437.2261@compuserve.com; Website: www.booksellers.org.uk. Price £50.

Directory of Publishing, Wellington House, 125 Strand, London WC2R 0BB. Tel: 020 7420 5555. Fax: 020 7240 8531 E-mail: casselladad@msa.com Website: www.cassell.co.uk

Publishers Handbook, Grosvenor Press, Tel: 020 7278 7772. Price £49.95. Covers services for publishers.

MDB Magazine Directory, 33–39 Bowling Green Lane, London EC1R 0DA. Tel: 020 7505 8000. Fax: 020 7505 8201. E-mail: andrewn@brad.co.uk

The Media Guide, eds Steve Peak and Paul Fisher, Fourth Estate, ISBN 1 84115 232 3

Small Press Year Book, National Small Press Centre, BM BOZO, London WC1N 3XX. Price £7.95.

National Small Press Centre Handbook – How To Self Publish from Bar Codes To Distributors, price £12. (For address, see above.)

Directory Publishing, a Practical Guide, by Russell A Perkins, MorganRand, ISBN 0 913061 01 8

Magazine & Journal Production, by Michael Barnard, Blueprint, ISBN 0 948905 01 8

The Smithsonian Book of Books, by Michael Olmert, Smithsonian Books, ISBN 0 89599 030 X

How To Market Books, by Alison Baverstock, Kogan Page, ISBN 0 7494 0126 5

Marketing for Small Publishers, by Keith Smith, Inter-Action Imprint, ISBN 0 904571 34 3

Marketing Without Money, by Nicholas E Bade, NTC Business Books, ISBN 0 8442 3343 9

DIY Direct Marketing, by Judith Donovan, Kogan Page, ISBN 0 7494 3304 3

Profit Through the Post, by Alison Cork, Piatkus, ISBN 0 7499 1313 4

Running Your Own Mail Order Business, by Malcolm Breckman, Kogan Page, ISBN 1 85091 213 0

Mail Order, a Small Business Guide, by Alan and Deborah Fowler, Sphere Books, ISBN 0 7221 3697 8

Ogilvy on Advertising, by David Ogilvy, Prion Books, ISBN 1 85375 196 0

101 Ways To Generate Great Ideas, by Timothy R V Foster, Kogan Page, ISBN 0 7494 0533 3

Choosing & Using Professional Advisors, by Paul Chaplin, Kogan Page, ISBN 1 85091 229 7

Magic Words That Bring You Riches, by Ted Nicholas, HiLite Ltd, ISBN 1 899 20502 0

The Neatest Little Guide to Making Money Online, by Jason Kelly, Nicholas Brealey Publishing, ISBN 1 85788 266 0

Journals

Book People, Chappell Thorne, 16 Chilham Way, Bromley, Kent BR2 7PR. Tel: 020 8462 9993. E-mail: bookpeople@chappell-thorne.com

Publishing News, 39 Store Street, London WC1E 7DB. Tel: 020 7692 2900. Fax: 020 7419 2111. E-mail: mailbox@publishingnews.co.uk

The Bookseller, 12 Dyott Street, London WC1A 1DF. Tel: 020 7420 6000. Fax: 020 7420 6013. E-mail: letters.to.editor@bookseller.co.uk

Comagazine, Tavistock Road, West Drayton, Middlesex UB7 0UE. Tel: 01895 433600. Fax: 01895 433602.

Magazine News, Queen's House, 28 Kingsway, London WC2B 6JR. Tel: 020 7404 4166. Fax: 020 7404 4167. Website: www.ppa.co.uk

The Magazine Business Weekly Report, Islington Business Centre, 14–22 Coleman Fields, London N1 7AE. Tel: 020 7688 6638. Fax: 020 7688 6637. E-mail: tmb@dircon.co.uk

New Media Age, 50 Poland Street, London W1V 4A. Tel: 020 7970 4000. Fax: 020 7970 4899. E-mail: mikeb@centaur.co.uk

Press Gazette, 19 Scarbrook Road, Croydon, Surrey CR0 1LX. Tel: 020 8565 4200. Fax: 020 8565 4395. E-mail: pged@qpp.co.uk

Publishing, 111 Upper Richmond Road, London SW15 2TJ. Tel: 020 8780 7800. Fax: 020 8788 2302. E-mail: forme@forme.com

Useful contacts and addresses

The following list is not meant to be exhaustive, but a starting point covering all sorts of areas relevant to small publishers, nor is inclusion in this list necessarily an endorsement or recommendation of the services offered, over which due diligence must be exercised.

www.dotgain.co.uk is a website dedicated to book production which enables publishers to get quotes from printers on-line, read the latest news from the book production world and browse a vacancy section devoted to book production.

T & A Typesetting Services, 189 Drake Street, Rochdale, Lancashire OL11 1EF. Tel: 01706 861662. Fax: 01706 861673. E-mail: a.edmondson@zen.co.uk

Small Print, The Old School House, 74 High Street, Swavesey, Cambridge CB4 5QU. Tel: 01954 231713. Fax: 01954 232777. E-mail: info@smallprt.demon.co.uk Small firm providing editorial, design, project management and audio production services.

Stephens Innocent, 21 New Fetter Lane, London EC4A 1AW. Tel: 020 7353 2000. Fax: 020 7353 4443. E-mail: nsoloman@ stephensinnocent.com
Solicitors specializing in copyright, publishing contracts and agreements and related matters.

Witan Publishing Services, Cherry Tree House, 8 Nelson Crescent, Cotes Heath, via Stafford ST21 6ST. Tel: 01782 791673.
Editing, proofreading, typesetting, design and advice on all aspects of publishing and marketing.

Wordwise Publishing Services Ltd, PO Box 88, Gosport, Hampshire PO13 9YT. Tel: 01705 359960. Fax: 01705 552950. E-mail: wordwise@ cix.co.uk Website: www.citsoft.co.uk/wordwise

Hans Zell, Publishing Consultant, 11 Richmond Road, PO Box 56, Oxford OX1 2SJ. Tel: 01865 511428. Fax: 01865 311534. E-mail: hzell@dial.pipex.com Website: www.hanszell.co.uk

GLOSSARY

A4 the size description of the standard paper used in photocopiers and laser printers. **A5** is half that size, **A3** twice the size

Advance a lump sum paid to authors at the commencement of a book contract or on delivery of the work. This sum is advanced against royalties and deducted from early royalties otherwise payable

Autoresponder a piece of software attached to a website that enables visitors to the site to download specific files like e-books when authorized (usually by the payment of a fee via credit card)

Back-end product a product which is offered to customers when or after they buy their first product. Back-end sales are crucial to the small publisher's profitability

Backlist the books previously published by a publisher and still available

Barcode a computer generated set of lines containing digital information (ISBN, price, etc.) that can be printed on the cover of a book or magazine

Buyers' list a mailing list of purchasers of a mail order product as distinct from a list of mere enquirers. Buyers' lists will produce much greater response for similar products and are likely to be more profitable despite higher cost

CD writer a CD-based drive on a computer which enables the user to load files onto a CD and to copy such CDs for distribution

Circulation the actual number of copies of a magazine or other serial publication that are sold or distributed (*see* **Readership**)

Comb binding a system of binding papers, usually with card covers in a spiral spine, usually of plastic

Compression large computer files such as e-books with graphics or other complex attributes can be compressed into .zip files by programs such as WinZip in order to shorten transmission time when delivered over the internet

Concatenation *see* **Funnel marketing**

Contents a listing at the front of a book giving an idea of the topics covered in the various chapters or sections

Conversion ratio the ratio of sales achieved from enquiries – normally around 20 per cent but can often be raised to more than 33 per cent by re-mailing the enquirers several times

Copyright ownership by writers and others of the intellectual rights to their work – lasts 70 years beyond the author's life

Copywriting the writing of sales letters and other written material designed to inform, persuade and sell

Correspondence or study course information published in sequential units and usually with a ring binder to contain them. Postal tuition based on set exercises is usually a feature of such courses

CRC (Camera Ready Copy) original text and artwork page layouts ready to go to the printers to be photographed onto the printing plates from which the publication will be printed

Database a collection of information, usually customer and prospect names and addresses, kept on computer

Data Protection Act an act laying particular responsibilities and obligations on anyone who keeps information or records of others either on computer or in the form of paper records

Direct mail the process of selling by mail sent to the customer's home or business as distinct from the more diffuse **mail order** which also encompasses selling via newspaper or magazine advertisements

Direct sales or **direct marketing** selling by advertisements or mailed letters or brochures direct to consumers or business clients in their own homes or businesses

Discretionary income income that is left over after basic needs are met which can, therefore, be spent on non-necessities

Distributor an agency or company that undertakes the process of getting books and magazines from publishers to the wholesale or retail outlets

Dropship a sales system on an agency basis where agents obtain sales, forward the orders to the publisher with the appropriate payment (usually 50 per cent), who sends out the goods direct to the customers. A useful way to increase sales or to increase what you can offer by dropshipping other publishers' products to your existing customers

DTP (Desk Top Publishing) a system whereby text can be prepared for books, magazines and other published items using a publishing program on a personal computer

Edition an updated version of a book

Editor the person in the publishing house with the responsibility for turning an author's work into a saleable publication. This is often specialized, with commissioning editors selecting works to be published, sub-editors checking the text for accuracy, style and grammar and so on

Electronic book or **e-book** – a book recorded as a computer file and presented either on a floppy disk, CD-ROM or as a downloadable internet file

Ephemera a collective term for short-lived, usually single sheet, publications such as postcards, posters, poem cards, etc.

E-zine a magazine published on the internet, often free and used to promote the purchase of other products

Facsimiles reproduction of exact copies of old documents and other original material

Fax-back a form of information publication by fax using an automated fax machine attached to a premium rate number

Floppy disk the $3^1/2''$ disks used in computers

Fonts or **founts** the individual design of the lettering chosen to make up the text

Footer text that is run along the bottom of each page, usually used for the page numbering

Footnotes notes on the text put at the foot of the page for easy reference, sometimes at the end of each chapter and sometimes in an extra section at the end of the book

Foreword an introduction to a book by an outside commentator or authority

Funnel marketing a progressive selling policy that begins with a free or low-cost product and attracts the customer to purchase increasingly more substantial and higher priced products

Glossary a listing, with brief explanation, of major terms used within a book and relating to the subject of the book

Gone-aways the names and addresses on a mailing list who are no longer at the address on the mailing label. These should be removed from your mailing list or returned to the company you rented the list from who should compensate you by supplying several new names for each undeliverable one you return

Goodwill deposit a system where an advertiser asks for a small returnable deposit as a gesture of good faith in return for a report, audio tape or other information pack about a high-priced product – the deposit is rarely reclaimed even if the enquiry proceeds no further

Gross profit the difference between the cost of goods and what you sell them at (*see* **Net profit**)

GSM the weight of paper (felt by thickness), 80 gsm being the standard copier weight and 100 gsm being preferred for quality work

Hardback a traditional book with stiff board covers and a paper jacket

Hardware in computer terms, the actual parts that make up the computer and associated accessories – hard drives, monitors, scanners, etc.

Header text that is run across the top of the page, usually the title of the work or chapter

Hot-melt binder a small, hand-operated machine which binds pages into special pre-glued covers to produce a simple manual

HTML the programming language used by professionals to create web pages

Imprint a name or brand under which a publisher brings out books or other published works

Independent publisher a publisher that is not part of a larger group or conglomerate

Index the listing of key words at the back of a book by page numbers for ease of reference

Infopreneur American term for an entrepreneur focusing on the sale of information

ISBN (International Standard Book Number) an officially assigned number which identifies a particular title

ISSN (International Standard Serial Number) an officially assigned number identifying a particular magazine or periodical

Issue refers to a current, past or future monthly, weekly or quarterly version of a magazine or journal

Justification in publishing terms this refers to the alignment of the text which is usually straight on the left and ragged at the right-hand side (**justified left**) or **justified**, which means that it is stretched the full length of the line to give straight margins on each side (though sometimes ragged white spaces among the print in the middle of the page), or **justified right** (rarely). Titles and some other material are justified by **centring** the text

Keying a system of tracking the results of advertising by always making it direct response and adding an identifying 'key' or code (a letter, name or symbol in the address) so that you can tell which advert provided the sale or enquiry

Leading refers to the space between the lines of type which affect appearance and readability

Legal deposit copies those copies of a published work which publishers are obliged by law under the Copyright Acts to deposit with the six major libraries in the UK

Libel defamation of a person in writing or other permanent form

Magazine normally a glossy, full colour weekly or monthly publication often covering very specific, but sometimes more general interests

Mailing list the in-house mailing list built up through advertising and capturing customers' names and addresses is the most valuable resource a small publisher can have and use

Mail order a well-established approach to sales direct to customers through advertisements or mailshots (letters and brochures) sent to their homes or offices

Mailshot or **mailing piece** a letter or a combination of letter, leaflet, brochure, return envelope, discount voucher, etc., sent out to prospective customers

Manuscript the written (seldom), typed or word-processed text from which a book originates. Also refers to articles submitted to a magazine or journal

Master tape the original high quality video or audio tape recording from which copies are made for sale

Masthead the title section of a magazine or journal which usually contains other information, such as the publisher's address and details, the editor and other staff, etc.

Minimum Terms Agreement preferred contract terms for authors drafted by the Society of Authors and the Writers Guild

Multi-media information products comprising several elements – print, audio, pictorial, video and film, etc.

Net profit what is left of your gross profit after you have taken off all the costs, such as rent, labour, sales and marketing costs, etc. (*see* **Gross profit**)

Newsletter a small serial publication simply and plainly produced (usually A4 in size) and circulated directly to subscribers or a membership

Newspaper although primarily a daily or weekly news-focused publication produced on newsprint in a tabloid or broadsheet size, sophisticated modern newspapers now carry a wealth of more general informational material on travel, fashion, the arts, sport and so on

Niche market an identifiable segment of potential customers for products narrowly targeted on their particular interests

Obscenity that which is likely to 'deprave and corrupt' others

Paperback a book with soft card covers and (usually) a glued spine – sometimes called a softback

Pareto principle the law formulated by Italian sociologist Vilfredo Pareto which broadly states that 80 per cent of results come from 20 per cent of the activity or the population under scrutiny

Part-work a publication focusing on a specific subject area in multiple format in which parts are released or mailed, usually on a monthly basis

PC personal computer

PDF file a computer file created and accessed for reading via the Adobe Acrobat software program which enables you to transfer the publication you have created to others via disk, CD or the internet so that they receive it in the exact form you created on your computer, including layout, colours, graphics, etc.

Personalized books this refers predominantly to books for children where the child's name and details are inserted to become part of the text of the story

PLR (Public Lending Right) a UK government scheme that makes funds available for writers and other creative contributors to have payments made to them from public borrowings from libraries

Point size the way in which the size of a typeface is measured. Most books, magazines and other published material are best set in 10 or 12 point type

Preface a brief note at the beginning of a book explaining its purpose, origin and so on

Prelims the preliminary pages at the start of a book, containing title page, bibliographical data, contents, etc.

Premium rate numbers revenue-producing telephone lines that can be used for publishing information

Press release a news item or short article announcing some newsworthy aspect of your publication or activities sent to magazine and newspaper editors who may run it as a news item – effectively free publicity

Pro-forma invoice an invoice sent and settled before the goods are dispatched

Proofs the typeset text in rough format for checking and correction

Publishing on demand producing information products by print or other means as and when orders are received

Qualified prospect an enquirer who has been screened or assessed in some way to determine their level of interest – perhaps by asking for a goodwill deposit (*q.v.*) or a couple of stamps to receive fuller information

Reader offers a method of getting free advertising by contacting magazine editors with bargain offers he or she can offer to the readers of their publication

Readership the number of people estimated to read a publication – generally reckoned (often optimistically) to be a multiple of two, three or more times the actual circulation (*see* **Circulation**)

Remainders books which the publisher has decided have reached the end of their shelf life. They are usually sold off to specialist remainder dealers, though often authors have a clause in their contract that gives them the first option of buying remainders of their books at a fraction of the cost

Remnant space advertising space that is available at the last minute before publication and can be obtained at huge discount by the tough-minded

Renewals the number of subscribers who pay for a further year's subscription to a magazine or newsletter

Reports (sometimes called manuals, guides or folios) short, often simply produced publications offering specialized information at a relatively high price and often produced by home publishers, sometimes under a reproduction and/or reprint licence

Reprints reproductions of out-of-print and/or out-of-copyright publications

Residual income income that comes in automatically without extra work having to be done to secure it, such as renewals to annual subscriptions, particularly if paid by direct debit or standing order

Resource box a panel or box at the end of an article, press release or report which gives your details for interested readers to follow up and contact you

Returns this has two meanings in publishing: the first is the system where retailers buy on 'sale or return', which means that you may get most of your stock returned for refund because the retailer did not sell it; the second refers to the return of a book or publication by a mail order buyer under the terms of your 'money-back guarantee of satisfaction'. While annoying, this system does at least increase initial sales from those potential customers who may be a little wary of sending off money to an unknown mail order publisher

Reversed out a print design in which white or coloured print is set against a black or other coloured background often making it difficult to read

Royalties sums paid on sales of an author's work based on an agreed percentage of sales

Sans serif a typeface style that lacks the embellishments of 'feet'. Though clear and modern looking and ideal for headlines and titles, it is not as easy to read as the more traditional serif typestyles

Secure website a site or part of a site that uses encryption of data to protect information such as credit card details, personal details, etc.

Self-publishing producing a book or other work written by oneself without the agency of a publisher

Serif a traditional type of typestyle with 'feet' – usually best for blocks of text

Shared mailings a means of cutting the cost of marketing by mail by sharing the expense with other non-competing businesses who want to reach the same prospects

Shareware computer programs that are made freely available to users who are then invited to pay a registration fee for continued use and updating

Shopping cart a website feature that enables you to click onto various products and bundle them together for purchasing

Short run publications books or other printed products produced in small quantities

Sidebar a box set at the side or in the middle of a page of text giving additional information to the main text – more commonly used in magazines and newsletters than in books

Slander spoken defamation of a person

Software the programs that make the computer work and perform special functions

Spin-offs additional revenue-creating opportunities and activities attached to a first sale or subscription-based publication – such as collections of 'The Best of …'

Spiral binding publications bound, usually with card covers, using a spiral spring to hold them together

Subsidiary rights publication rights for other countries or media other than that in which a book or other work is originally published

Two-step marketing a mail order approach using small (usually classified) advertisements or brief flyers to solicit enquiries and following up with full information packs about the product

Typesetting the process of turning a typed or word-processed manuscript into the kind of type appropriate for a book or magazine. Formerly done with physical lead type by hand or using a typesetting machine, this is now done electronically

USP (Unique Selling Proposition) the unique quality or benefit your company or product offers

Vanity publishing this is quite distinct from self-publishing, an honourable path for authors, but is an exploitative business where vanity publishers advertise for new authors, tell them their work is wonderful and charge them vast sums to produce a few copies while making little or no effort to sell them

VAT (Value Added Tax) a tax levied on most goods and services. Most printed and published goods are exempt if less than 25 per cent is designed to be written on. At the time of writing the lower limit for registration is a turnover of £50,000 – as a publisher of books and magazines with a smaller turnover it may be worth registering in order to reclaim tax paid on purchases

Voice over a commentary spoken, recorded and played over a filmed sequence

Wire binding the trade term for stapling in booklet format

INDEX

TEACH YOURSELF

JOURNALISM

Geoff Pridmore

With the vast steps in communication technology taken during the last century, the role of journalists has never been so important or so challenging.

Teach Yourself Journalism is a practical introduction to this exciting – and competitive – career, which offers enormous opportunities for those who succeed.

Covering all areas of journalism, from freelancing to internet journalism, this book gives you:

- Practical information on getting a foot in the door
- Detailed coverage of each type of journalistic career
- Advice on training, finding work and career progression.

Geoff Pridmore is a freelance journalist and teacher. As a student, he was a winning finalist in BBC Radio 4's feature making competition – 'Fresh Air Media'.

Other related titles

TEACH YOURSELF

COPYWRITING
SECOND EDITION

J. Jonathan Gabay

Fully revised for today's practical copywriting requirements, *Teach Yourself Copywriting* reveals some of advertising's greatest creative secrets.

From planning to implementation, it will guide you step-by-step through copywriting skills for a range of disciplines, including:

- The Internet
- Radio and TV
- Business-to-business
- Public relations
- Recruitment
- Charities

'Plenty of nuggets and well worth keeping close to hand for inspiration'
INSTITUTE OF DIRECT MARKETING

'Perfectly explains how copywriting works'
DAILY TELEGRAPH

'Compulsory and compulsive reading'
JAMIE DOW, BRAND DEVELOPMENT CENTRE

J. Jonathan Gabay is an award-winning copywriter, Course Director at the Chartered Institute of Marketing, the world's biggest marketing training organization, and director of a creative marketing consultancy firm.

TEACH YOURSELF

FREELANCING

Ros Jay

Going freelance has a lot of appeal, but if you can't make a living at it you simply can't afford to do it. *Teach Yourself Freelancing* prepares you for the pitfalls and equips you with the skills you need to succeed as a freelance.

The book:

- covers everything from how to set up as a freelance, find new clients, manage your time, set your prices and keep your accounts, to how to market yourself
- includes a self-assessment questionnaire to see if freelancing is for you
- is full of practical tips and techniques.

Ros Jay is a professional freelance writer and editor who has written several business books, including *Teach Yourself Marketing your Small Business*.

TEACH YOURSELF

MARKETING YOUR SMALL BUSINESS

Ros Jay

Teach Yourself Marketing Your Small Business is designed for people starting up or already involved in running a small business. Focusing on the type of marketing relevant to small businesses, it looks at:

- brainstorming your market plan
- public relations
- corporate image
- advertising
- exhibitions
- direct mail
- selling and customer care
- keeping to a budget

A freelance business writer and editor, Ros Jay writes in a clear, jargon-free language, and includes checklists, practical exercises, easy-reference summaries and lists of 'Dos' and 'Don'ts' to give a comprehensive introduction to marketing a small business.

TEACH YOURSELF

BOOK-KEEPING AND ACCOUNTING FOR YOUR SMALL BUSINESS

Mike Truman

This clear and practical book provides guidance on how to keep the books and prepare the accounts for your small business. Forget about debits and credits, journal entries, ledgers and day books – if you can read a bank statement this book will teach you how to prepare accounts for tax purposes and for the bank manager, how to make forecasts of your cashflow, and how to prepare a budget for your business.

With completely up-to-date information, the book follows the layout of the Inland Revenue self-assessment tax return for preparing accounts. Step-by-step coverage of book-keeping and accounting makes this an accessible and invaluable guide for small business needs.

Mike Truman is a Chartered Accountant and a Fellow of the Chartered Institute of Taxation, as well as being a professional writer in accountancy and taxation.